Apprenticeship Launch System™

How to Start Apprenticeships without the Red Tape, Even If This Is New to You

Andy Seth

Disclaimer

The information provided in this book is intended for general informational purposes only. While every effort has been made to ensure the accuracy and reliability of the information presented, laws, interpretations, and guidance on rules and regulations change frequently. Therefore, I make no representations or warranties of any kind, express or implied, about the completeness, accuracy, reliability, suitability, or availability of the information contained herein. I disclaim any liability or responsibility for any errors or omissions in the content of this book. Your use of the information contained herein is at your own risk.

This book is not intended to be a substitute for professional advice specific to your circumstances. For tailored guidance and support, please reach out to Apprentix, where we specialize in helping businesses navigate these complexities.

ISBN: 979-8-9918861-1-6 (paperback)

Guiding Principle

Apprenticeships must lead to business growth.

Table of Contents

Section I: Start Here

Welcome to the Apprenticeship Launch System™ (ALS™). When I first started creating apprenticeships within my own companies, I couldn't believe that no one had written down how to make them successful by driving business growth—not just the broad strokes, but the details only an operator would know. To this day, there hasn't been a single book that lays out the details of launching an apprenticeship program. Till now.

I've spent the past year pouring everything I know into this book and being absolutely secretive about the stuff that I'm going to share with you. The whole point of ALS is to make apprenticeship knowledge accessible to everyone. That's why I've written this book: so that, hopefully, more businesses run apprenticeships and use apprenticeship programs as a way to grow their business and do great things in the world.

Occasionally, some of you may say, "Yo, Andy, can we run our apprenticeships on your platform, Apprentix?" And I'll say, "Yes, you'll love it." If you are a business leader and you're thinking about starting an apprenticeship program or must start one because of a government-backed program, the first thing you start with is knowing how to launch such a program. Far too often, businesses launch apprenticeship programs and fail. That's a bad look for you and the apprentices. I want to help you avoid that and get you prepared so that you're successful.

Where does this book fit into the Seth School, if you will? ALS answers the question "How do I launch an apprenticeship?" Once you know how to launch an apprenticeship, the next question is "How do I operate an apprenticeship?" That's where the Apprenticeship Operating System™ (AOS™) comes in.

How to **_launch_**? ⟶ ALS™   How to **_operate_**? ⟶ AOS™

If your apprenticeships directly lead to business growth—let's say you use them to acquire new customers, start new projects, or have an unlimited talent pool—you can continue to win new business and deliver your services over and over again. Having this single skill is one of the biggest business-insurance activities you could possibly undertake, because once you have this humming, you won't ever do without it again.

The problem is this: starting an apprenticeship is overly complicated and filled with red tape, and people who haven't ever run a business or apprenticeship are supposedly the ones to tell you how to run yours. These people don't understand the dynamics of business leaders running a company, working a full-time job, bringing in revenue, making sure you're delivering what was promised, and treating your crew with respect—even if you don't always get it in return. They can't relate to the everyday demands of the business leaders.

It's easy to bark in writing, but real life isn't the same. I aim to solve this with ALS. This is the process of knowing what to expect in advance and launching your apprenticeship program in thirty days or fewer—guaranteed.

How I Got Here

Now for a quick story. Back in 2015, I exited a wealth management business that I had built to manage over $100 million in assets in nine years, and I wanted to do something that was good for business while being a force for good in the world. I didn't want to do some cheesy gimmick, like a buy one, get one free deal. I wanted to truly bake the good into my business model, and I just couldn't come up with how. I came across a white paper that had been published earlier that year by the Center on International Educational Benchmarking titled "Gold Standard: The Swiss Vocational Education and Training System."[1] It opened my eyes to a world that could be, but not only that—it was a world I had experienced personally.

I never really knew the word *apprentice* in this context because I'd always been told to go to college when, in fact, I had been an apprentice myself and had employed people who were apprentices. So I decided to start a business that would employ apprentices. And I'll tell you a little bit about how that went.

I went to the apprenticeships.gov website, and let me tell you, it was a bunch of psychobabble. It is to this day. Go check it out if you want. I then called my state apprenticeship office and asked them for help, and I quickly learned how full of red tape they were and how little they truly understood about the operations of an apprenticeship.

---

[1] Nancy Hoffman and Robert Schwartz, "Gold Standard: The Swiss Vocational Education and Training System" (Washington, DC: National Center on Education and the Economy, 2015).

Actual Transcript of the Call to the Apprenticeship National Contact Center

Agent: Thank you for contacting the Apprenticeship National Contact Center. How may I assist you today?

Me: On the website at apprenticeship.gov, there are two different options for starting a new apprenticeship. On one page, it says that my options are to create a registered apprenticeship program or an industry-recognized apprenticeship program. And then on a separate page, it says that my options are to create a program or join an existing program. Am I first deciding on registered versus industry, or am I first deciding on creating my own or joining an intermediary?

Agent: Right now, sir, basically we give you just the proper information, and I'm trying to look for a phone number where you can go ahead and call and they can go ahead and answer that question for you. But unfortunately, sir, I don't have that information.

Me: So where do I go to ask about how to start an apprenticeship?

Agent: It's not giving me any phone numbers here, sir. It's only giving me websites.

Me: But what do I do now?

Agent: I wouldn't know, sir. Honestly.

What? There's nowhere to go, and I hadn't even gotten past step one. That's what's happening, and we have millions and millions of dollars going out to fund apprenticeships—and I can't even start one. That's the problem we've got right now, and that's the problem I want to solve, because this is ridiculous.

After months of back and forth, no-shows to meetings, and a frustrating experience, I said, "Forget it. I'll do it myself." I started a business and hired my first employee, who was an apprentice. I must admit, I was nervous because I was taking a huge risk. Imagine, who makes their first employee an apprentice? Someone who basically doesn't know what to do. And here's the thing: I was totally alone and unplugged from any type of support system.

I took the leap and decided to start my own apprenticeship program, and I decided not to register it. I figured I'd just take the leap and get going. The bureaucrats weren't any help anyway, so it was better that I took action and learned on the job. Well, when I had my first prospect meeting, I told them about our apprenticeship program. They loved the idea that they could get all the services they needed delivered and could support an apprentice in building their career. I did this over and over again, selling deals and delivering services with the use of apprentices. Not the entire service but a piece of the service was delivered with apprentices. All those apprentices are here in the United States.

My leadership team loved the mission but was finding it hard to create new apprenticeships as we grew, and then to manage them. So I went on the search for a solution. I tried all kinds of different tools. I tried a project management system that's not designed for apprenticeships at all. I tried a customer relationship management, or CRM, tool. That didn't work. I even tried buying an apprenticeship management tool that was on the market, but it was clearly built by bureaucrats who cared only about registered apprenticeships and compliance reporting. They didn't know what it takes to operate an apprenticeship program, so it just looked like a tool that was meant for reporting.

During COVID, I apprenticed myself under a master coder and taught myself how to program software. My project was to build a tool that could help my team create apprenticeships from scratch and register them automatically, almost like TurboTax does for tax prep, and then to build apprenticeship management tools that are made for operators, not just for compliance reporting.

Every single line of code in Apprentix has my experience built into it as someone who has launched and operated apprenticeships at scale. When it was time to launch our beta version, I hoped to have a few companies willing to take a look and give me feedback. Three thousand organizations applied to our wait list. Of these, 48 percent of them were businesses like us, and the remainder were organizations that I hadn't actually built this for: they were intermediaries, unions, education providers, associations, workforce boards, and state agencies.

When the bureaucrats found out that I was allowing apprenticeships to be launched and operated without being required to register with the state, they were pissed. They turned their backs on us during meeting after meeting and told us that if we didn't make our platform exclusively for registered apprenticeships, they wouldn't support us. Can you imagine that? We built a solution that businesses lined up for in the thousands, something no bureaucrat had ever come close to achieving, and they turned their backs on us because we allowed the market to freely choose what was best for it in terms of registering apprenticeships or not. Rather than give in to their demands, we doubled down on our approach, allowing every type of work-based learning opportunity on our platform, from registered and unregistered apprenticeships to internships and externships to upskilling and reskilling. We now have more apprenticeships on Apprentix than almost every state in the US has.

I've packaged up all the knowledge I've gathered in launching hundreds of apprenticeship programs, and I'd like to share this one skill with you. I have some flaws, and I have made my fair share of mistakes, but I can teach you how to launch apprenticeships that generate a return on investment. I can't make the decision for you to launch an apprenticeship, but I promise I won't let you fail.

I also want to thank you genuinely. Thank you for allowing me to do work I find meaningful. Thank you for lending me your most valuable asset: your energy. I promise to do my best to give you the highest possible return on your apprenticeships. This book delivers.

Businesses need more skilled talent. They need less bureaucracy. And that's what I promise you—apprenticeships without the bullshit.

The Problem This Book Solves

Apprenticeships offer a unique blend of hands-on experience and structured learning that's hard to beat. For businesses, they provide a pipeline of low-cost, skilled labor tailored exactly to the needs of the business. Think about it: you get to train someone from the ground up, ensuring they fit your company culture and processes perfectly.

On the flip side, apprenticeships aren't just about cheap labor. They're about investing in people, fostering loyalty, and reducing turnover. You're not just hiring employees—you're building a dedicated workforce.

However, it's not all smooth sailing. The red tape and initial setup can be daunting, and without the right approach, the costs can outweigh the benefits. This book aims to cut through the bureaucracy and show you how to make apprenticeships work for you, efficiently and profitably. So if you're intrigued by the idea of apprenticeships but unsure about the hurdles, keep reading. We'll turn those hurdles into stepping stones.

The Problem

One of the biggest concerns businesses have when launching any new initiative is the cost and burden being added to the organization. Launching an apprenticeship program is no exception. To make matters worse, apprenticeships are often filled with psychobabble and red tape, guided by bureaucrats who haven't run a business, let alone an apprenticeship, themselves. As a result, businesses struggle to win more projects and deliver them with a homegrown talent pool of skilled labor. Brutal! This means less money and talent flow to the business.

So now that you know you have a problem, unless you're allergic to making money and helping people, you've gotta solve it.

The Solution

To launch an apprenticeship program that grows your business, you must do two things:

1. Keep it low cost.

2. Cut the red tape.

That's it. I've launched apprenticeships within my portfolio of companies with this exact framework and have helped hundreds of businesses do the same. ALS focuses on profitable apprenticeships. You drive profitability by doing the following:

1. Building a training program

2. Not changing the way you work

3. Training low-cost labor

4. Selling work at a higher price

5. Graduating labor into skilled roles

6. Having these employees teach the next cohort

The Bottom Line

All else being equal, when you win projects and deliver them with low-cost labor being trained by in-house experts, you increase your profit.

This book shows you how to transform your business into an endless pool of talent to deliver high-margin work. Once you apply its models, you *instantly* increase the skills your business needs. And when you have people who can actually do the job, it's hard not to make money. This book will solve your not-enough-people problem for good.

The bottom line? I'll show you how to start apprenticeships without the red tape, even if this is new to you.

What's in It for Me?

In one word: **trust**.

I provide this book and the course that comes with it for free (or at cost) in hopes of earning your trust. By offering you more value than any government-funded agency, $30,000 consultant, or $100,000 apprenticeship coordinator, I aim to support businesses like yours in launching successful apprenticeships.

This isn't just about the money—it's about building a relationship with you and sharing Apprentix as a tool that can genuinely help you succeed. Trust is the foundation of this relationship, and through this book, I want to demonstrate my commitment to your success. I have a different model, which I explain below.

I want to provide value to two types of businesses: those that want to launch apprenticeship programs for *themselves* and those that oversee or support apprenticeships for *other businesses*.

If you want to launch an apprenticeship program for your own business, my goal is to get your program launched within thirty days and, in doing so, *earn your trust.* I'm putting all of that together for you here, for free. My hope is that you can take what I've learned and accomplished and do it for yourself. And in doing so, if you decide to use Apprentix to launch and operate your apprenticeships, then I'll have accomplished my mission, which is to use my business as a force for doing good and to spread the power of apprenticeships throughout the United States.

The second type of business is one that oversees or supports apprenticeships for *other businesses.* This includes everyone who helps other businesses meet apprenticeship labor requirements, from an intermediary who works with multiple employers to a construction contractor and their subcontractors. If this is you, it would be my honor to help you launch and scale your program.

I don't sell coaching, masterminds, courses, or anything like that. I provide education, technology, and services to businesses that need to launch apprenticeships that succeed.

My Business Model

My business model is simple:

1. Provide better free products than the government or the paid products on the market.

2. Earn the trust of businesses launching and running apprenticeships.

3. Provide education, technology, and services to fast-track their growth.

4. Help everyone else for free and use business as a force for good.

Our process ensures success by being thoroughly tested and proven. Businesses know my models work because they've experienced their effectiveness firsthand. And I trust that businesses will use these models because they are practical and results oriented. This mutual trust is the foundation of our shared success.

This approach avoids failures and increases the likelihood of success. Win-win. Easy to say, but let me show you how much of a difference our process makes.

Within the **first thirty days, our average customer launches a custom-designed apprenticeship program** that doesn't require them to change the way they work, is low cost, and cuts all the red tape. For those required by law to use registered apprentices to bid on projects, **within ninety days, our average**

customer is winning once-in-a-generation wealth-building projects. This stuff works.

That's how I know the models I'm about to show you work. *They already have.*

Apprentix's Mission

To help businesses grow through the power of apprenticeships.

Businesses solve the world's biggest problems. There simply aren't enough skilled workers to help businesses solve these problems, and that leads to stagnant innovation and growth.

My Personal Mission

I love this country, and I don't want to see us falling behind. But unless we get back to our roots of unskilled labor being trained by masters of their craft, we're simply not going to have the people to do the work, and businesses will not grow as much as they can. That means fewer Americans building once-in-a-generation wealth, fewer Americans in the middle class, and fewer Americans getting out of poverty.

I grew up the son of Indian immigrants in a Los Angeles motel that we didn't own, where I lived till I was fourteen. My parents were part of the working class. I went to a military academy, became an apprentice, and started my own business. God has blessed me in my career, and I feel fortunate to have been given this mission: to help people grow profit and purpose.

Basic Outline of this Book

I laid out this book to help you start an apprenticeship from scratch—zero experience, zero skills, and zero apprentices. This book also reminds those of us with existing apprenticeship programs, me included, of the basics we stopped doing or that we overcomplicated. *Our businesses depend on us to do better.* Just like a master tradesperson still does the basics, so must we.

So we go from designing your first apprenticeship program to launching one. Here's the breakdown:

- Section I: *You're reading it right now.*

- Section II: Deciding on Registered vs. Unregistered Apprenticeships

- Section III: How to Create Apprenticeships from Scratch

- Section IV: How to Register Apprenticeships and Stay Compliant

GOLDEN TICKET

We work with businesses with new and existing, registered or unregistered apprenticeship programs. If you would like us to help launch or scale an apprenticeship program, go to **Apprentix.io**. You can also find **free** books and courses so good they'll help you take advantage of apprenticeships to grow your business. And if you're not a fan of typing, you can scan the QR code below to grab them.

SCAN ME

Alpha Program Blueprint

I'm going to start by showing you how to define your first apprenticeship program's goals and how to extract the value from it. I say *extract* because you must mine it, just like anything of value. A gold miner cannot succeed if he digs where there is no gold. A farmer cannot succeed if he plants crops where there is no sun, water, or nutrients in the soil.

Bureaucrats think apprenticeships are inherently valuable to businesses. But they know nothing about running a business. They know nothing about profitability. Do not launch an apprenticeship guided by bureaucrats and end up with nothing to your name.

A business can create an apprenticeship program, but their program will remain unsuccessful because they're too unaware, too uneducated, to know where to mine. Identify where the value drivers are before you launch. This section will teach you where to mine.

Pick up that shovel—it's time to dig in.

What Is Your Compelling Reason for Launching an Apprenticeship Program?

The first thing I want you to ask yourself is **"What is my compelling reason for starting an apprenticeship program?"** The reason I use the word *compelling* is that this must be an initiative in your business that compels you to move forward. This must be a driving force behind your business. It cannot just be a little one-off project that you just take on because it sounds cool.

I've run apprenticeship programs in my own businesses, having started them from scratch to do good for the community. That was the wrong approach. Turns out, my apprenticeship programs needed to drive business value, and the side benefit was that they would help people and they would help the community. But I needed it to work for the business; otherwise, it wasn't sustainable. And I made the mistake myself in trying to design something that was diverting some of our profits away simply to do some good, and that wasn't the right approach. That's what I want to help you avoid.

You are not here to just design something that provides a good reputation for your brand or reflects some corporate social responsibility that builds your reputation in the community. That's not what we're here for. We're here to give you tangible results because you have an apprenticeship program. That's the focus here. If your focus isn't that, then I don't think having an apprenticeship program is worthwhile because it will become an investment that will eventually be cut. And that, in fact, will be more harmful to the community than had you not started one to begin with. Your community starts to depend on businesses that have work-based learning opportunities, and businesses start to build that reputation. When businesses do away with their apprenticeships program, their street cred takes a hit. "Oh, they couldn't hang; they couldn't sustain this." And that's worse for your reputation. That's why we're going to focus only on the goals that will drive business results.

Identifying Key Value Drivers

To truly extract value from your apprenticeship program, you must identify the key value drivers that align with your business's unique needs and goals. This section will guide you on where to mine for those drivers to ensure your apprenticeship program delivers significant returns.

Winning New Business

One of the most compelling reasons to implement an apprenticeship program is its potential to help you win new business. Many public projects and large contracts now require companies to have apprenticeship programs in place as part of their bid criteria. Notable examples include the following:

- **The Inflation Reduction Act**, which incentivizes the use of apprenticeships to qualify for certain clean energy project credits. Businesses in the renewable energy sector can secure substantial tax benefits by integrating apprenticeship programs into their projects. (Learn more about the Inflation Reduction Act's apprenticeship requirements in my course at https://www.iracompliance.co.)

- **The CHIPS and Science Act**, which requires semiconductor manufacturers to have apprenticeship programs to receive federal funding. The goal is to build a skilled workforce to support the booming semiconductor industry in the US.

- **The Bipartisan Infrastructure Law**, which includes various provisions that favor companies with robust apprenticeship programs when bidding for federal infrastructure projects. It aims to create pathways into good jobs in sectors such as transportation, water infrastructure, and broadband.

- **The National Apprenticeship Act of 2023**, which seeks to create nearly one million new apprenticeship opportunities over the next five years by investing more than $3.8 billion. It supports expanding apprenticeships into new and in-demand industries, ensuring that businesses with registered programs are well positioned to win contracts and funding.[2]

By integrating apprenticeships into your business strategy, you can meet these requirements and position your company as a preferred bidder, thereby increasing your revenue and market share.

Upskilling and Reskilling

Upskilling your workforce is a primary driver of value. This involves training your existing employees to take on higher-level roles within your company. By promoting from within, you not only fill these critical roles but also ensure that the employees moving up already understand your company culture and processes. Upskilling leads to a more capable and motivated workforce that is ready to take on greater responsibilities.

Let me give you an example. One of Apprentix's customers is a hospitality company with thousands of employees, most of whom are frontline workers. They faced a significant challenge in hiring enough first-level managers for various reasons, such

---

[2] House Committee on Education and the Workforce, "National Apprentice Act of 2023" (fact sheet, Ed & Workforce Democrats), https://democrats-edworkforce.house.gov/imo/media/doc/national_apprenticeship_act_of_2023_fact_sheet.pdf#:~:text=URL%3A%20https%3A%2F%2Fdemocrats; Education & the Workforce Committee Democrats, "Labor Leaders Introduce Bipartisan Bill to Expand Apprenticeships," news release no. 202-226-0853, April 25, 2023, https://democrats-edworkforce.house.gov/media/press-releases/labor-leaders-introduce-bipartisan-bill-to-expand-apprenticeships; White House, "Biden–Harris Administration Announces Strategies to Train and Connect American Workers to Jobs Created by the President's Investing in America Agenda," fact sheet, May 16, 2023, https://www.whitehouse.gov/briefing-room/statements-releases/2023/05/16/fact-sheet-biden-harris-administration-announces-strategies-to-train-and-connect-american-workers-to-jobs-created-by-the-presidents-investing-in-america-agenda/.

as a limited supply of qualified candidates at an affordable price point and the need for specific training tailored to the business's unique requirements. To address this, the company implemented an unregistered apprenticeship program to upskill the best, brightest, and hardest-working employees who want to enroll. The apprentices receive free education and skills training in exchange for being promoted and making more money.

The result has been outstanding. They graduate over 90 percent of their apprentices into management roles, with each cohort consisting of nearly fifty people—a number that continues to grow with each new cohort they launch. By upskilling their workforce, this hospitality company has not only filled critical management positions but has also ensured that these new managers were already familiar with the company's operations and culture. This internal promotion strategy has created a motivated and skilled management team, driving the company's success.

An upskilling apprenticeship doesn't mean it's just for new and young employees. You can upskill to any position. I have seen Apprentix customers upskill employees into the C-suite!

This can even be important for companies looking to reskill people. Maybe a group of people will lose their jobs or need to be repositioned. You can reskill them using an apprenticeship, since it's simply a path to get someone from job A to job B, and it can go all the way across and up your organization. You can put any type of apprenticeship on Apprentix and operate it right there on that platform. It doesn't have to be a new hire, and it doesn't have to be a government-registered apprenticeship focused on entry-level positions (a subject we'll cover in more detail later). In the real world, you can make any job apprenticeable.

Providing Cost-Effective Training

Another significant value driver is cost-effective training. When companies approach the state to start an apprenticeship program, they often follow the path of building a registered apprenticeship because the state works only with registered apprenticeships. The state does not help companies set up unregistered apprenticeships, even if that's best for the business. As a result, the state agency will look for training providers within the system and recommend courses provided by external providers, which cost the business a lot of money. The state does this because it is feeding its ecosystem, which is filled with organizations that all live off government funding.

From a business standpoint, it is much smarter to provide as much of the training as possible in-house, provided it meets the business's needs. When training is developed internally, the cost of the training curriculum drops to $0, and it can be tailored specifically to the business's requirements. The business would purchase training from a third party only if it couldn't deliver that training in-house. This leads to a much more cost-effective training approach and one that is completely tailored to the business. We cover this in the "Coursework Designer" chapter.

Let's consider another Apprentix customer, a manufacturing company that initially approached its state agency to set up an apprenticeship program. It was directed to expensive external training providers within the system. Recognizing the high costs, the company decided to look for an alternative solution and came across Apprentix. We guided the company's managers to develop most of their training in-house, so they created a custom curriculum tailored to their specific processes and equipment. This in-house training approach significantly reduced costs and ensured that apprentices learned exactly what was needed for their roles. As a result, the company saw a substantial increase in productivity and a higher return on investment in its apprenticeship program.

Apprenticeships allow you to provide structured, in-house training instead of sending employees to expensive external programs. This means you can tailor the training to meet your specific business needs and ensure that your employees gain the exact skills required for their roles. Effective training programs minimize downtime and maximize productivity, leading to significant cost savings and higher returns on your investment in human capital.

Building a Talent Pipeline

Building a talent pipeline is about creating a steady stream of skilled workers from within. If you're struggling to hire skilled people and end up in a bidding war with competitors, an apprenticeship program can help. Instead of poaching talent and squeezing your margins, invest in people and train them to do the job you need. It might take time—maybe six months or even three months—but it doesn't have to be four years unless that's what the program requires. You have a choice: either engage in bidding wars or create a program that builds your own talent.

Another Apprentix customer success story: A tech company found it difficult to hire experienced developers and was constantly facing high hiring costs. By establishing an apprenticeship program with Apprentix, management brought in junior developers and individuals with a strong interest in tech. Over a few months, they trained them on their specific tech stack and methodologies. This approach saved the company from the high costs of hiring experienced professionals and ensured that the new hires were well integrated into the company's culture and processes, making them more effective and loyal employees.

One common concern is that after investing in training, employees might leave for competitors offering higher pay. While this risk exists, the benefits of building a talent pipeline often outweigh this concern. Here are a few ways to address this issue, drawing on strategies used by companies with tuition reimbursement programs:

1. **Retention strategies.** Implement strong retention strategies, such as career development opportunities, competitive compensation, and a positive work environment. Employees are more likely to stay with a company that invests in their growth and offers a clear career path.

2. **Employee contracts.** Like tuition reimbursement programs do, use contracts that require employees to stay for a certain period after completing their training. For example, employees might be required to stay for two years after training or repay a portion of the training costs if they leave early. This can help protect your investment.

3. **Reimbursement agreements.** Establish agreements that include repayment clauses for training costs. If an employee leaves within a certain period after receiving training, they must repay a portion or all of the training costs. This creates a financial incentive for them to stay.

4. **Continuous development.** Keep investing in your employees' development. When they see ongoing opportunities for growth and advancement within your company, they'll be less tempted to jump ship for a competitor.

5. **Company culture.** Foster a company culture that values loyalty, engagement, and employee satisfaction. When employees feel valued and connected to the company's mission, they're less likely to leave.

6. **Clear career paths.** Like tuition reimbursement programs do, clearly outline the career advancement opportunities available to employees who complete the apprenticeship program. Show them the tangible benefits of staying with the company long term.

Building a talent pipeline means you're constantly nurturing and developing talent from within. This proactive approach helps you stay ahead of your staffing needs, ensures a good cultural fit, and significantly reduces hiring costs. It's about planning and securing a reliable supply of skilled workers who are ready to step into roles as your business grows.

Increasing Retention

Increasing retention is another goal. Employees often leave for slightly higher pay, and you wonder, "Why would you leave? We have a great culture, we care about you, we invest in you." Yet they leave for a small increase. This problem is frustrating. Research shows that replacing an employee can cost 50 to 60 percent of their annual salary, with total costs ranging from 90 to 200 percent of their salary.[3] This problem is especially significant in trades, where the demand for skilled labor is high. For example, the construction industry had 374,000 job openings as of December 2023.[4] Retention is critical. Additionally, the Inflation Reduction Act is expected to boost renewable energy jobs significantly, with projections indicating the creation of

---

[3] Steven Austin, "The High Cost of Employee Turnover: Causes, Benchmarks, and Reduction Strategies for 2024," Marketing Scoop, May 12, 2024, https://www.marketingscoop.com/marketing/the-high-cost-of-employee-turnover-causes-benchmarks-and-reduction-strategies-for-2024/; Kate Heinz, "38 Employee Turnover Statistics to Know," Built In, last updated by Brennan Whitfield on April 17, 2023, https://builtin.com/recruiting/employee-turnover-statistics.

[4] Ezra Greenberg, Erik Schaefer, and Brooke Weddle, "Tradespeople Wanted: The Need for Critical Trade Skills in the US," McKinsey & Company, April 9, 2024, https://www.mckinsey.com/capabilities/people-and-organizational-performance/our-insights/tradespeople-wanted-the-need-for-critical-trade-skills-in-the-us.

hundreds of thousands of new positions by 2030 as a result of increased investments in solar and wind energy projects.[5]

How does an apprenticeship help? It shows employees a clear path to advancement. If you tell someone, "Here's what you need to learn to make more money," they're more likely to stay. They see you investing in them, which fosters loyalty. It's important to communicate this directly: "We're investing in you because we value you, and we hope for your loyalty in return."

Boil all the strategies down and it's quite simple: your employees want to know what they need to do to make more money. An apprenticeship makes that answer crystal clear for them. By providing a structured pathway for skill development and career progression, apprenticeships make it clear how employees can advance and increase their earnings. This transparency reduces the allure of leaving for a marginally higher salary elsewhere. Employees feel valued and see a future with your company, which is crucial for maintaining a stable and committed workforce.

Creating Redundancy

Creating redundancy involves transferring knowledge from experienced workers to new ones. This is essential, especially given the current labor shortage in the trades. Let's paint the picture: There's a 1.57 million shortfall of skilled tradespeople due to a lack of new entrants and many professionals retiring. Trades are often perceived as less desirable, noncareer, minimum-wage positions, which deters potential entrants. As a result, many current trade professionals are nearing retirement without enough

---

[5] "Inflation Reduction Act Will Attract an Extra $270 Billion in US Wind and Solar Investments by 2030," Rystad Energy, August 22, 2022, https://www.rystadenergy.com/news/inflation-reduction-act-will-attract-an-extra-270-billion-in-us-wind-and-solar-in.

new workers to replace them. Consequently, fewer skilled professionals are purchasing and using products from major retail and supply brands.[6]

The situation is not just limited to the trades. By 2030, manufacturing alone will have 2.1 million openings. The Bipartisan Infrastructure Law is expected to peak around 2027–28, potentially expanding the job market by 345,000 positions across various sectors. Additionally, the renewables industry will require an estimated 1.1 million blue-collar workers by 2030 for the development and maintenance of wind and solar plants.[7]

Retirement is going to widen this gap even further. Nearly one in four construction workers is over fifty-five years old, meaning a significant portion of the workforce is nearing retirement. This is particularly concerning because many of these older workers are highly skilled and productive. For example, 30 percent of union electricians will reach retirement age in the next decade, and this figure could be indicative of other occupations and nonunion shops.[8]

Now let's talk about rural areas. There are incredible businesses in rural communities where the owner is ready to retire but has no one to take over. If you were willing to approach the owner, learn from them, and commit to building a life in that community, there's a good chance you could buy the business. You could structure the deal in a way that helps the owner retire and makes it affordable for you

[6] John D. Campbell and James V. Reyes-Picknell, *Uptime: Strategies for Excellence in Maintenance Management* (Boca Raton: CRC Press, 1995), https://vdoc.pub/documents/uptime-strategies-for-excellence-in-maintenance-management-2k63kstqup3g.

[7] Paul Daume et al., "Renewable-Energy Development in a Net-Zero World: Overcoming Talent Gaps," McKinsey & Company, November 4, 2022, https://www.mckinsey.com/industries/electric-power-and-natural-gas/our-insights/renewable-energy-development-in-a-net-zero-world-overcoming-talent-gaps.

[8] Campbell and Reyes-Picknell, *Uptime*.

to get started. As the new owner, you'd be training an apprentice to take over your business, and that apprentice could be someone who already works for you.

Consider the massive hassle when someone leaves your company for another job. You must find someone else, train them, interrupt your ongoing projects, and disrupt your team's workflow. Turnover has a huge cost on your ability to hit your numbers. Training apprentices for redundancy means preparing people to step into roles if someone leaves. This is huge for your business because you'll have a bench of talent ready to go.

If you have employees who've been with the company for years, an apprenticeship can ensure their skills are passed on to newer employees. This continuity is crucial for the business's success. By having a system in place where seasoned workers mentor apprentices, you maintain the flow of knowledge and skills within your company, ensuring you're never left in the lurch when someone retires or moves on.

Incorporating apprenticeships to build redundancy not only secures your business's future but also strengthens it. You create a robust talent pipeline that can fill in gaps, adapt to changes, and sustain growth. It's about planning and making sure you're always prepared, no matter what challenges come your way.

Expanding Hiring Pools

Expanding your hiring pools is a valuable strategy for finding potential apprentices who may not come from traditional career paths. By adopting skills-based hiring practices, you can cast a wider net and attract individuals with the right abilities, regardless of their formal qualifications or previous job titles. This approach not only increases your chances of finding talented and motivated apprentices but also brings in fresh perspectives and innovative ideas. Focusing on skills rather than credentials allows you to tap into a broader and more diverse talent pool, ultimately strengthening your workforce and enhancing your company's adaptability.

Pro Tip: Use Apprentix to Automatically Generate a Skills-Based Job Description

To help you expand your hiring pool, Apprentix automates 100 percent of the skills-based job description for you. All you have to do is type in a job title—there are over 57,000 different job titles on this platform—and it will spit out a skills-based job description for you. You can use this for every single job there is. You can edit it, delete it, what have you, but it will spit out a skills-based job description for you.

By focusing on these key value drivers—winning new business, upskilling and reskilling, cost-effective training, building a talent pipeline, increasing retention, creating redundancy, and expanding hiring pools—you can ensure that your apprenticeship program delivers maximum value to your business. Remember, the goal is to align the program with your specific business needs and objectives, turning it into a powerful tool for growth and success.

Section II: Deciding on Registered vs. Unregistered Apprenticeships

If you can't explain it simply, you don't understand it well enough.

- Albert Einstein

Bureaucrats want you OVERWHELMED. They want you to simultaneously accept that apprenticeships are complex ecosystems that cannot be navigated without them while also having you believe that the process is simple enough for anyone to manage on their own. Bureaucratic psychobabble isn't just about verbal efficiency or camaraderie. It's about power. The more cryptic the jargon, the more the newbies will feel disempowered.

This is about taking the power back. Making the difficult feel easy.

Now that you've defined your apprenticeship's goals, the roles needed to launch the program, and how to assemble all the pieces from this book to launch an apprenticeship that drives business results, we will dive into the next question: should you register your apprenticeship program or not?

We will start with giving you the options you have to create and run an apprenticeship program, including what's in it for you and for the apprentice, what it means to register your program and some of the challenges registration entails, why these programs fail, and what it takes for them to thrive. Hopefully, you will be clear on whether registering an apprenticeship program makes sense for your business.

Giddy up.

The Apprenticeship Myth

Let's bust a myth that's causing more harm than good, especially for small businesses. It's the idea that you must have a *registered* apprenticeship program (RAP) filed with the Department of Labor (DoL) or state agency or it's not a "real" apprenticeship. This is nonsense, and we need to pump the brakes on it.

Many businesses fall into this trap, thinking:

1. "I need government funding to offset program costs."

2. "I need government resources for recruitment."

3. "I need a registered program to be legitimate."

For most small businesses not required to have a registered apprenticeship, this is overkill. You'll waste time and money working within a bureaucratic system that imposes requirements and costs that funding won't offset. The compliance headache isn't worth the meager support they offer. Plus, you're sacrificing the freedom to run your apprenticeship as you see fit.

My advice? Save your time and dollars. Invest in an apprenticeship that trains your people and grows your business.

Now, if you're legally required to have a registered apprenticeship program, I've got you covered. I'll dive into those specifics in Section IV. If you don't need a registered program, feel free to skip it or cherry-pick useful bits for your apprenticeship.

Let's get into the six essential things you need to know before launching an apprenticeship program. This knowledge will help you avoid costly mistakes that often lead businesses to give up and lose millions.

The Essential Six

The six essential things you must know before starting an apprenticeship program are what an apprenticeship is, both to the apprentice and to the business; what a registered apprenticeship is; who has these programs; why businesses don't start them; why apprenticeship programs fail; and why yours can thrive.

1. What Exactly Is an Apprenticeship?

An apprenticeship is one thing from the apprentice's point of view and another from the business's, so let's look at both sides as well as the historical precedent.

Historical Origins of Apprenticeships

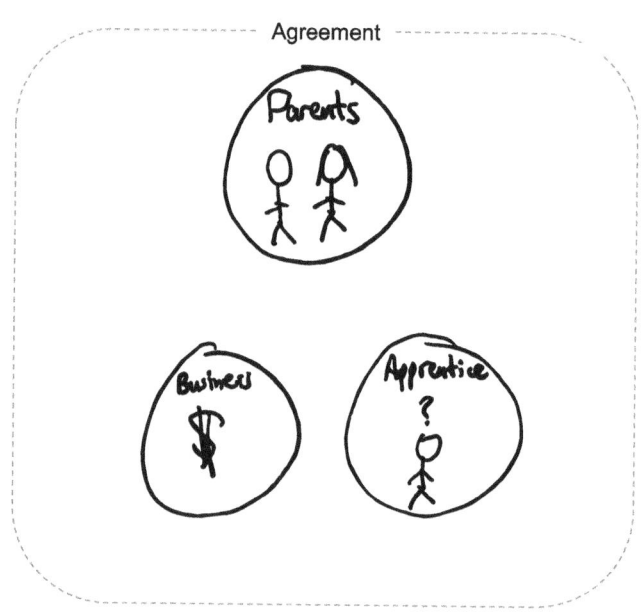

Apprenticeships were agreements in the form of an indenture, which was effectively a contract between the parents, business, and apprentice, with a tear-off sheet to match the papers between all parties. Parents would go to businesses and basically say, "Hey, we've got this kid who doesn't know how to do much. Can you teach them what you know how to do so that they have some skills and can eventually have a job that makes money and maybe even a business like you one day?"

The business owner would say, "What's in it for me?" And the parents would say, "Okay, how about this? You have to pay them barely anything, so they're going to be low cost. You train them to do exactly what you need for your business so that they're doing the work you need and helping you generate profit, and you can continue to focus on bringing in more customers." Effectively, that was the arrangement, and in exchange, the parents said, "We promise that if our child doesn't complete their program and doesn't make you the money that you invested in them, we'll pay you back."

The business looked at this and said, "This is a pretty fair deal. I can get somebody cheap. I can train them up. Once I've trained them up, they can move on and do whatever they want. But in the meantime, I've got some inexpensive labor, and it's somebody who's going to know exactly how to do the job I want to have done. And maybe they'll move on, but maybe they'll stay with my business and help me and continue to work with me." And that happened quite often. From a business perspective, it was also a solid deal.

From the kid's perspective, becoming an apprentice was a good deal too because now they would learn a skill. They would learn some competencies that would get them somewhere in life, give them a profession, a path to money, and a potential path to their own business. It was a good deal. Of course they were going to work for very little—they knew they didn't know much. "Yeah, that's totally doable. I don't mind working for a little bit of money."

That's why apprenticeships were a solid deal, because it had this three-way dynamic. And you already know what the parents were thinking: "Hey, business owner, take care of our child. Hey, kid, see you on the other side. We'll celebrate when you've finished your apprenticeship. See ya—we're gone!"

From the Apprentice's Point of View

To an apprentice, an apprenticeship program has four core elements: it's a paid job that provides on-the-job training, classroom instruction, and mentorship.

What is an apprenticeship?

TO AN APPRENTICE

Paid jobby job	**On-the-job** training
Classroom instruction	**Mentorship** support

Paid Jobby Job

An apprenticeship means that it's a paid jobby job. The apprentice must be employed; it's a full-time job. Think of it this way: The apprentice has a job and is enrolled in an apprenticeship program, much like someone who has a daytime job and attends night school. But unlike night school, where the job and school are distinct, an apprenticeship integrates both aspects more deeply. The apprentice's job and their educational program are intertwined. They learn on the job and might also take classes after work. This integration is deeper and more cohesive than the separation you'd find in a traditional job-and-night-school setup. So in the case of an apprenticeship, it is, first and foremost, a paid job.

This distinction is important because it helps you understand that if somebody doesn't fit or doesn't do the work as an apprentice, the business can terminate their apprenticeship program but can keep them as an employee. It's not that the person has to be terminated completely from employment. The business can simply terminate the apprenticeship program itself.

Classroom Instruction

Apprenticeships require apprentices to receive classroom instruction. That classroom instruction could be online, in person, or a hybrid of both. Classroom instruction might take place before apprentices start working, in the form of an orientation. Classroom instruction can also take place while apprentices are working on the job. In this case, they usually have certain days or blocks of hours during which they're in class versus when they're working on the job, or they might take some courses after work, or both. It depends on how the company itself structures it, but classroom instruction is a part of an apprenticeship, so there's actual formal training.

Here's why: How do you get an apprentice to "get it"? For them to get it, they have to understand the theory, the concepts. You don't want to waste time on the job to explain concepts while they're supposed to be learning how to do something. That's why classroom instruction is important.

On-the-Job Training

On-the-job training is important because that's what teaches them how to do the work. Just because you know how to do something in theory doesn't mean you know how to do it. Said another way, **just because you learned it doesn't mean you can do it**.

(Say it louder for the people in the back!)

Though classroom learning is important, it's not nearly as crucial as on-the-job training. When you look at the weekly ratio, an apprentice works forty hours but spends only a few of those in the classroom. This clearly shows that the emphasis is on practical, hands-on experience. They need those classroom hours to understand the concepts and truly get it, but most of their learning happens while working.

Mentorship Support

The final component of an apprenticeship for the apprentice is mentorship support. They have someone who's been there, done that—often called a journeyman, though it could be anyone a level above them who knows the job inside and out. This mentor teaches them what they need to know to do the job. And that's really what an apprenticeship is for the apprentice. Most people stop here when describing an apprenticeship program, seeing it as something only for the worker.

But we're going to go one step further. What exactly is an apprenticeship program for a business?

From the Business's Point of View

What is an apprenticeship?

TO AN APPRENTICE		TO A BUSINESS	
Paid jobby job	**On-the-job** training	**Low-cost** labor	**Trained** to your needs
Classroom instruction	**Mentorship** support	**Gets** it	**Reduced** turnover

Low-Cost Labor

To a business, an apprentice is low-cost labor. Let's make no mistake about this. The point of a business investing in someone is that they get them at a low cost upfront and over time make investments in that person as their productivity increases. Then they potentially give them more money. But the whole point of this is that it is low-cost labor that's legal. Why is that important? Because businesses make their money on people. That is one of the ways that they leverage human capital.

For a business to invest in someone to develop them, the worker must start at a rate that is commensurate with their skill level. For somebody who doesn't know much, that's going to be a low rate, so it is a low-cost labor play.

Gets It

One of the biggest challenges in running a business, speaking as an entrepreneur myself, is that the business needs people who not only match its values but who also have what's called GWC:

- Gets it

- Wants it

- Has the competency for it

One of the things that you must teach as a business is the "gets it" part. You really need the apprentice to get it. You want the apprentice to understand what it is they're doing and, conceptually, what their job will look like. If they do not understand the actual components of the job, how their work contributes to the bigger picture, and how the bigger picture contributes to the company's overall success, they're going to be out of alignment. If they're out of alignment, they're not going to be productive workers. So from a business's point of view, an apprenticeship is providing someone with instruction so that they get it.

Trained to the Needs of the Business

The third part is you, the business, get someone who's trained specifically on your needs. This is important because it means you don't have to hire somebody from the outside who will typically cost more money and who doesn't necessarily have exactly the right skill sets or the same skill sets or the level of skills you would like in that person. With an apprentice, you can train that person up so that the apprentice has exactly the skills the business needs.

When somebody is trained specifically to your needs, you can have someone do everything you need done without paying for a whole lot of waste. Think of it like this:

If you're looking for somebody who has a list of twenty skills and they walk in with a list of twenty skills but only fifteen of those skills match, you have five skills you're not using and five skills you need to train on. Therefore, that business is saying, "Okay, I've gotta train them on these five things, and if they now have these five things, they complete the list of twenty skills I need to get our job done. And I'm paying for those other five skills but really don't need them."

Businesses are looking for skill matches with the jobs they need performed, and with apprentices, they can make exact matches.

Reduced Turnover

By investing in a mentor and providing apprentices with support and teaching them the ropes, along with making a big investment in the actual worker, the business achieves retention. This is an important factor because retention is difficult to achieve, especially when you're talking about businesses that have the types of jobs where people tend to bounce around from company to company in exchange for just slightly higher pay. By investing in an apprentice, a business is saying, "Look, I'm going to make an investment in you, but you have to stick around a little bit longer." Hopefully, the apprentice looks at it and says, "Yeah, this is actually a fair deal for me."

It all seems pretty simple, right? But it's not so simple when you talk about a registered apprenticeship program. Oh, a registered apprenticeship program is a whole different beast. Let's dive into what exactly a registered apprenticeship program is.

2. What Is a Registered Apprenticeship?

Remember my fancy drawing where I showed you the agreement between parents, businesses, and apprentices? Over time, the government took the place of parents. In return, they changed the system.

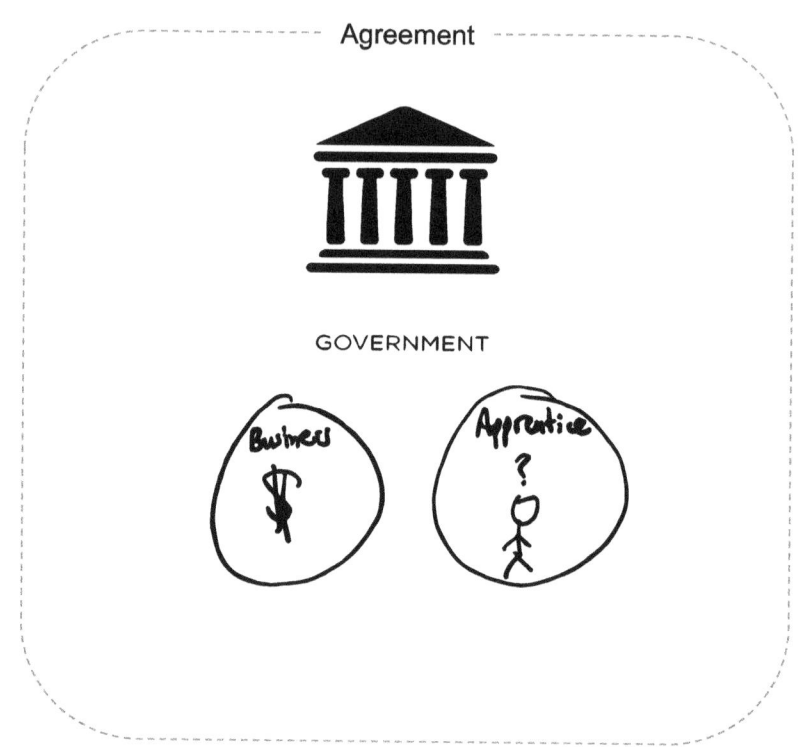

They created a whole other system that went from being something pretty simple in nature to something pretty complex. We're going to dive into what makes this complex. This will help you understand all the ins and outs to avoid the types of issues or confusion that often arise when a business goes down the registered apprenticeship route.

First, the government treats things differently than parents did. For one, and this is something that rubs me the wrong way, they changed the terminology from *businesses* to *employers*. Like that's the entire function of a business—to employ people. Well, let me tell you, that is not what a business is in business for, and I think it's important to understand this because one of the mistakes that businesses make, and that bureaucrats advise them on, is that they look at themselves as employers. Being employers is not their primary function.

Peter Drucker famously said, "**Businesses are in the business of creating and keeping customers.**" Without customers, businesses have no revenue. Without revenue, there are no employees. Once we understand that registered apprenticeships use a different language, we can start to understand how things have shifted from the old-school focus on parents to a focus on the government.

Second, the apprenticeship agreement itself is no longer between parents and businesses. Now it's an agreement between the DoL and the business in which the business agrees to provide training. In exchange, what does the business get? Well, we'll find out what they get. But what I can tell you is they don't get a whole lot for their money. This is a controversial viewpoint because everyone pushes registered apprenticeships, but the reason they push registered apprenticeships is because *they are funded by the government.*

My company, Apprentix, is not funded by the government, so I can say whatever I want, and I can tell you that half of the apprenticeships on our platform are NOT registered apprenticeships. There's a reason for that, and we're going to get into that in just a bit.

Let's look at what a registered apprenticeship requires that standard apprenticeships don't: to be part of a specific occupation, include wage bumps, and require certain hours and credentials.

Apprenticeable Occupation

To create a registered apprenticeship, the occupation must be on the DoL's "Apprenticeable Occupations" list. When they say it's an apprenticeable occupation, what they really mean is "We can register it because it's already on the list of apprenticeships that we have registered in the past." If it's never been apprenticed before and it's a brand-new occupation, you have to take a whole other—lengthy—registration path, but we won't get into that just yet. What I will tell you is that if it's on the apprenticeable occupation list, it means it's already been done and they already understand it, so you can register your program under the umbrella of that occupation.

Wage Bump

There has to be at least one wage bump along the way and one upon graduation. An apprentice in your company without a registered apprenticeship can make whatever money you're willing to negotiate and they're willing to accept, and you pay them as you will, when you will. It's good to give them a bump along the way if they're being productive for you because it encourages them to continue to stay with you and to move along, but you're not required to.

In a registered apprenticeship, you must have at least one wage increase while they're in the apprenticeship itself, and they must make more money when they finish it. Typically, they're moving from apprentice to the actual job, so it's going to make sense that you'd have one wage bump upon graduation, but that additional wage bump within the apprenticeship itself is a unique feature of registered apprenticeships.

Minimum Hours Required

Registered apprenticeships must be a minimum of two thousand hours, basically one year. That means an apprenticeship of only three months or six months can't be a registered apprenticeship. There is no way to make that happen because the government says that a registered apprenticeship must be at least one year.

Now, you might hear other people saying, "Well, that's not true if you have a pre-apprenticeship." Let me tell you something. A pre-apprenticeship is not an apprenticeship. The reason is that it fails to meet criterion number one. A pre-apprenticeship is not a job. A pre-apprenticeship is a training program. It just contains the term *apprenticeship*, so it can be a bit confusing.

Credentials

A registered apprenticeship must lead to the apprentice earning an industry-recognized credential. What's an industry-recognized credential? That usually means the DoL issues a certificate that says, "Congratulations! Because you've gone through this program that we have recognized in the past as an apprenticeable occupation and you have now completed it, we, the DoL, will issue you the certificate." That's what it typically means. Does that carry a lot of weight in the marketplace? Absolutely not. Not for most businesses—they don't really care.

There are trades, for example, that do understand apprenticeships well because they've been around forever. They understand that if somebody walks in with the DoL certificate as an apprentice, it means something, but typically, outside of that, they won't recognize it. Not that they won't honor it—I just mean that they don't get it. Companies aren't in the business of knowing that the DoL issues certificates. Is it industry recognized? Maybe. Depends on the industry. There are other credentials the apprentice could earn from third-party education providers, so those types of credentials are also issued when the apprentice finishes.

Now that we've unpacked what a registered apprenticeship involves—its ins and outs and the hoops you must jump through—it's clear why this path is so popular in industries like construction, where unions play a big role, and with European companies, especially German ones. But don't overlook the fact that nearly half of all apprenticeships are unregistered. These programs offer a ton of flexibility, letting you design shorter, more tailored experiences that suit your specific needs without the bureaucratic hassle. As you weigh your options, keep in mind that both registered and unregistered apprenticeships have their own sets of benefits and challenges. The key is to pick the one that aligns with your business goals, industry demands, and how much red tape you're willing to deal with.

3. Who Actually Has an Apprenticeship Program?

Deciding whether to go with a registered or unregistered apprenticeship program is all about what fits your business best. Registered apprenticeships come with a stamp of approval and some government perks, but they also drag you into a maze of red tape. Unregistered apprenticeships, on the other hand, give you the freedom to shape the program as you see fit without getting bogged down by regulations. Knowing who typically runs these programs and what's happening in the apprenticeship landscape today will help you make the smartest choice for your business.

Let's start by looking at registered apprenticeships. According to "The Role of Trade Unions in the US Apprenticeship Arena" by Franklin Apprenticeships, 70 percent of registered apprenticeships are in construction.[9] This probably comes as not too much of a surprise if you've been around apprenticeships for a while, because apprenticeships really started and have grabbed hold in the construction space. Construction continues to be the number one place where apprenticeships are. Franklin Apprenticeships goes on to say that 80 percent of those construction apprenticeships are run by unions. Thus, the concentration of registered apprenticeships is both in construction and within the unions that run them for those businesses.

Obviously, 30 percent are not in construction. According to Ryan Craig's *Apprentice Nation*, most of those non-construction apprenticeships are run by

---

[9] Franklin Apprenticeships, "The Role of Trade Unions in the US Apprenticeship Arena," transcript of interview with Dr. John Gaal, https://www.franklinapprenticeships.com/role-trade-unions-us-apprenticeship-arena/.

subsidiaries of German companies.[10] You might be thinking, "Why German companies?" It's because the Germans have strong apprenticeship programs, as do other European countries such as the United Kingdom, Switzerland, and Austria. But the German subsidiaries continue with their apprenticeship programs here in the United States, so most of the non-construction apprenticeships are run by subsidiaries of German companies—a little-known fact. There are other companies that run apprenticeship programs, but the majority are run by German companies.

Now let's look at unregistered apprenticeships, which are just apprenticeships, but I'm going to use the term unregistered to make the differentiation here. According to Robert Lerman in "The State of Apprenticeship in the US: A Plan for Scale," there are half a million unregistered apprentices in the nation.[11] This is important to understand because in total we're talking about one million apprentices nationwide. Out of that, half are in the programs that are tracked by the government, but there's a whole other half that are not in these registered apprenticeship programs. This is important to know if you're considering starting or running an apprenticeship program, because all the news and all the information and the people who are touting apprenticeships are pushing toward registration. It's often forgotten that almost half are not registered apprentices.

This research is supported by my own data within Apprentix, where just over 50 percent of the apprenticeships on our platform are unregistered. Even though every customer on Apprentix goes through the process of creating a high-quality

---

[10] Ryan Craig, *Apprentice Nation: How the "Earn and Learn" Alternative to Higher Education Will Create a Stronger and Fairer America* (Dallas: BenBella Books, 2023).

[11] Robert Lerman, "The State of Apprenticeship in the US: A Plan for Scale," Apprenticeships for America. July 2022, https://static1.squarespace.com/static/61f1c7ff7041697cc1eff1bd/t/62d5b4981261b74803071036/1658172568403/planforscale.pdf.

apprenticeship program and could register their apprenticeship with the literal click of a button, they choose not to. The reasons vary, but in general, unregistered apprenticeships give businesses a whole lot of flexibility. For example, you can make them shorter than one year, whereas a registered apprenticeship must be at least one year.

Understanding who typically runs apprenticeship programs and the current landscape gives you a clearer picture of the practical implications. Registered apprenticeships dominate fields like construction, primarily driven by unions and large European companies. However, don't ignore the flexibility and customization that unregistered apprenticeships offer. They allow you to tailor the program duration and structure to fit your specific business needs without the heavy regulatory burdens. Ultimately, the choice between registered and unregistered apprenticeships depends on your business goals, industry standards, and how much bureaucratic hassle you're willing to deal with.

4. Why Don't Businesses Start Registered Apprenticeships?

The number one reason businesses don't have apprenticeship programs is because of the cost of registered programs and the lack of understanding that you don't have to go that route. Let's look at the cost drivers of registered apprenticeships, which include hiring or assigning program sponsors and administrators, recruiting apprentices, ensuring on-the-job training, developing and delivering classroom instruction, paying for mentor time, paying apprentices and giving wage bumps, and requirements related to registering an apprenticeship program.

Hiring or Assigning a Program Sponsor

When you have a registered apprenticeship program, there's a role called a program sponsor, and that person has a whole string of ongoing responsibilities, including compliance and ensuring that the program is meeting the standards that have been registered with the DoL or the state. You're either going to have to hire someone for this role or assign someone internally.

Hiring or Assigning a Program Administrator

You'll also need to hire or assign someone to be the program administrator, or program admin. The admin is different from the sponsor because they have different responsibilities. Some companies can get away with hiring one person to be both the sponsor and the admin. In either case, they have to invest in human capital to oversee a program, so there's a large cost just in human capital there.

Recruiting and Screening High-Potential (But Untrained) Talent

There's of course the recruiting and screening of the apprentices. What's interesting about this is that yes, apprentices might be high-potential candidates, but they aren't really trained yet, so they're going to enter at a low cost. Recruiting a low-cost hire is a bit of an out-of-balance investment because there's a large investment in recruiting someone who is also then a low-cost employee at first.

Ensuring There's an On-The-Job Training Aspect to the Work

You must ensure that there's on-the-job training in the work itself. When someone is training on the job, both the apprentice themself is not productive and therefore not making the company money *and* the person training them is not doing the work they're supposed to be focused on because they're busy training the apprentice.

Developing and Delivering a Curriculum for Classroom Instruction

What is it that's going to be taught? What does that curriculum look like? How do you develop that or potentially purchase that? Courses can be done online or delivered through a community college, but there's a cost to that as well. And then there's of course the cost of the training itself. Are they training while on the job? Are they training after? Are you paying for their time to do that?

Assigning Mentors and Paying Them (Presumably Extra)

Running a high-quality mentorship program requires a business to scope out the mentoring process, assign mentors to apprentices, teach mentors the skills needed to work with apprentices, and pay mentors for the time spent with apprentices.

Hiring Apprentices and Paying Wages as They Ramp Up

This entails the actual hiring of apprentices and paying their wages as they continue to increase their productivity and having those wage increases. So there are the wage bumps that must occur as well, and that's an added cost.

Requirements of Registering the Program with the DoL or State

Registering the apprenticeship program with the DoL or the state involves time and resources, and the process is full of red tape. Here's a breakdown of what you need to do:

- **Apprenticeship agreement.** You'll need a signed agreement between the apprentice and your business. This agreement details classroom and on-the-job training, wage progressions, and the overall structure of the apprenticeship, such as the training approach, duration, and probationary period.

- **Selection procedures.** Define how apprentices are selected, ensuring compliance with equal opportunity and affirmative action plans. You can't discriminate based on race, gender, age, ethnicity, religion, or disability.

- **Defined term of apprenticeship.** You must specify the length of the apprenticeship. Typically, this is a minimum of two thousand hours, but it could be longer—three thousand, four thousand, or even eight thousand hours. Alternatively, for a competency-based apprenticeship, the focus is on skills rather than time, allowing apprentices to progress as they demonstrate proficiency. However, not all trades are eligible for this model, so you'll need to check if your trade qualifies.

- **Work process.** Clearly outline what the apprentice needs to learn and how they will learn it. This means defining the specific skills and tasks they'll master throughout the program.

- **Apprentice-to-journey-worker ratio.** The ratio of apprentices to experienced workers or journey workers is regulated. You don't get to decide this on your own; the government sets this ratio to ensure proper supervision and training.

- **Apprentice wage schedule.** You'll need to lay out the starting wage, the final wage, and the increments for wage increases. This should reflect the apprentice's progress and training milestones.

- **Classroom instruction outline.** Define what will be taught, how it will be taught, and the curriculum. Whether you handle the instruction internally or purchase it from an external source, you need a clear plan.

- **Monitoring and documenting progress.** Develop a plan to monitor and document the apprentice's progress. This includes tracking compliance, progress reviews, and ensuring that the apprenticeship standards are met throughout the program.

- **Probation and termination policies.** After the probationary period—typically 25 percent of the apprenticeship's total duration or no more than one year—

you cannot terminate an apprentice without cause. This is different from at-will employment and requires careful consideration.

Businesses shy away from registered apprenticeships primarily due to cost and complexity. From hiring program sponsors and admins to developing a curriculum and ensuring compliance, the expenses and logistical hurdles can be substantial. Many companies find the process too burdensome and opt for the flexibility of unregistered apprenticeships. In both cases, they find the use of Apprentix to be key to staying organized and streamlined. By knowing these cost drivers, you can make a more informed decision on which path to take, balancing the benefits against the investments required.

5. Why Do Apprenticeships Fail?

Even with the best intentions, apprenticeship programs can hit significant roadblocks. Whether registered or not, they face challenges that can derail their success. From my private conversations with state apprenticeship training representatives (ATRs), I estimate that at least 5 percent of registered apprenticeships deregister each year. Let's break down the reasons for this so that you can avoid making the same mistakes:

- **Lack of business growth.** One of the main reasons apprenticeships fail is that they don't help grow the business. Businesses need to create customers to generate revenue and margin, which in turn funds the apprenticeship program. If the program doesn't contribute to acquiring new projects or creating a talent pipeline, it's not seen as beneficial. Without these business outcomes, companies are likely to deregister their apprenticeships.

- **Not in the training business.** Many businesses aren't prepared to handle the extensive training required by an apprenticeship program. It takes a lot of time and effort to administer, sponsor, and oversee the program. Employees who manage the apprenticeship often have other responsibilities, making it hard to maintain the program effectively.

- **Turnover of program champions.** Often, a passionate individual starts the apprenticeship program. If this person leaves, the program can suffer because the remaining staff may not share the same enthusiasm or understanding. This lack of continuity can lead to the program's collapse.

- **Little to no support.** Government agencies provide technical assistance, but this usually just means connecting you with resources rather than offering hands-on help. This lack of practical support means businesses are left to manage complex programs on their own, leading to frustration and potential failure.

- **Compliance challenges.** Compliance is a significant issue. Keeping up with regulatory requirements, maintaining updated databases, and ensuring all standards are met can be overwhelming. Noncompliance, especially on government-funded projects, can result in steep penalties, adding to the burden.

- **Failure to live up to the hype.** Apprenticeships can sound appealing, but if they don't deliver visible success, they quickly lose their charm. Success breeds excitement and validation, but without meeting business objectives, the program can feel like it's all hype and no substance.

- **Loss of grant funding.** Many apprenticeship programs rely on grant funding to offset costs. When this funding dries up, the programs often do too. If a program is heavily dependent on external funding, its sustainability is always at risk.

- **People problems.** There are often challenges related to the apprentices themselves, such as personal issues affecting their work, or journey workers who aren't committed or capable trainers. Additionally, instructors might not feel it's their responsibility or prefer other work, creating further obstacles.

Apprenticeship programs, whether registered or not, can face a bunch of hurdles that can cause them to fail. From not driving business growth and the heavy lifting required for training to the loss of key champions and the maze of compliance, there are plenty of reasons these programs can go off the rails. Knowing these pitfalls is your first step in avoiding them. While it might seem like a lot to manage, addressing these challenges head-on will help you build a strong and effective apprenticeship program.

I know what you're thinking: "Dang, Andy, that's a whole lot of reasons these things don't work." I know. Don't be dismayed. Let's talk about what makes some apprenticeships thrive and how you can apply those winning strategies to your own business.

6. Which Apprenticeships Thrive?

What is it about some apprenticeships that makes them succeed? As we've seen, there are plenty of obstacles, but the few that succeed and use this as a strategic advantage to their business have figured out some crucial elements. There are three key principles behind each successful apprenticeship program. Let's walk through them one by one.

Principle 1: Grow the Business

The first principle is that they focus on growing the business. Successful programs set clear objectives for the apprenticeship and track them rigorously. They often focus on the following:

- **Business growth.** Many apprenticeships contribute to winning new public projects that require apprenticeship programs, thereby increasing revenue. For example, a construction company might secure government contracts by incorporating apprenticeships into their bids.

- **Talent growth.** Programs are designed to upskill current employees and recruit new talent. This helps build a pipeline of skilled workers tailored to the company's needs. A manufacturing firm, for instance, might use apprenticeships to train workers in specialized skills, reducing the need for external hires and ensuring a steady flow of capable employees.

Tracking the efficacy of these programs involves scorecards and feedback loops:

- **Scorecards**—monitoring metrics such as the number of new projects won due to apprenticeship requirements or the improvement in employee retention and productivity

- **Feedback loops**—regularly gathering feedback from apprentices and mentors to refine and improve the program

Principle 2: Keep It Low Cost

The second principle is to keep it low cost. Think of the term *minimum viable product* (MVP), which is used in technology and product development. An MVP is the simplest version of a product that can be released to test and learn from customer feedback with minimal effort and resources. Similarly, successful apprenticeship programs invest just enough to achieve their results without overstaffing, overcommitting resources, or overspending. They focus on the essentials needed to run the program effectively, allowing you to test and iterate without excessive financial risk.

Principle 3: Cut the Red Tape

The third principle is cutting through the red tape. There's a tremendous amount of bureaucracy involved in setting up and running an apprenticeship, but successful programs figure out the workarounds. They streamline processes, automate where possible, and navigate the system effectively. Understanding how to work within and around bureaucratic constraints is vital. These programs don't just comply—they optimize, making the system work for them instead of getting bogged down by it.

We've broken down what makes apprenticeships successful by focusing on business growth, keeping costs low, and cutting through the red tape. These principles are key to creating a program that not only survives but thrives. The goal is to leverage apprenticeships as a strategic advantage, helping your business grow and ensuring a steady flow of skilled workers tailored to your specific needs. With these insights, you're ready to build an apprenticeship program that's both effective and sustainable.

When Do You Need a Registered Apprenticeship Program?

Now let's get into when you really need a registered apprenticeship program. There are only two main reasons: because you must comply with regulations and because you want to tap into funding opportunities. If your projects require compliance, particularly publicly funded projects, then a registered apprenticeship is mandatory. On the flip side, if you're seeking grants or tax incentives, a registered apprenticeship becomes a crucial metric for tracking and reporting success. Let's dive into the details of these two scenarios.

1. **You must comply.** If you need to be compliant to work on certain types of projects, typically publicly funded ones, you must have a registered apprenticeship program. For example, under the Inflation Reduction Act, if you're working on any clean energy projects, an apprenticeship program is mandatory. Similarly, if you're working on a publicly funded project in Denver, there's a law requiring an apprenticeship program. California has similar regulations. This requirement exists across the United States at federal, state, and local levels. If compliance demands a registered apprenticeship program for publicly funded projects, you can't use an unregistered one. Even if the regulations don't always specify, when they do, you will need a registered apprenticeship program.

2. **You want funding.** If you are seeking grants, tax incentives, or public funding, you must create a registered apprenticeship program. This is because registered programs provide the metrics needed for tracking and reporting against their grants. Think of it like this: If the government is going to give you money, they

need to show results, such as the number of new jobs created, people completing apprenticeships, and businesses running apprenticeship programs. These metrics are essential for their grant reporting. They will say, "We're giving you this money, but we need to see the outcomes."

If you run your own program and don't report it, the government can't count those metrics, which means they can't report the impact of the grant funding. Without these reports, they can't secure more funding in the future. That's the game they play. Their revenue comes from requesting money, whether it's at the state or federal level, from us, the taxpayers. This money circulates through grants, which require outcome reports to justify future funding.

The grant-funding world operates like businesses, which aim to serve their customers well to earn referrals and grow their reputation. Similarly, grant-funding organizations need to demonstrate success in their previous grants to obtain new ones. How do they prove that? By ensuring you report data through the registered apprenticeship program so they can count it.

* * *

We've covered a lot of ground in this section to help you understand more specifics about the options you have to create and run an apprenticeship program, including what's in it for you and the apprentice, what it means to register your program, the challenges registration entails, why these programs fail, and what it takes for them to thrive. Armed with this knowledge, you're better equipped to make the right choice for your business. Remember, the goal is to create an apprenticeship program that trains your people effectively and drives business growth—whether it's registered or not.

Now let's dive into the practical aspects of designing your apprenticeship program, applying the insights we've gained here. Hopefully, it will encourage you to take the plunge. Next, we discuss how to design your program for success.

Section III: How to Create Apprenticeships from Scratch

This is the meat-and-potatoes section of the book where I'll walk you through how to design an apprenticeship program that doesn't change the way you work . . . or at least, not much.

The key to apprenticeship design isn't what the bureaucrats tell you—they're focused on every way an apprenticeship is supposed to benefit the apprentice. The key to apprenticeship design is this: the apprenticeship program must fit neatly into your business so that it's easily operated. Once you have a well-designed apprenticeship that can be easily operated, you can mine it for profit. Only *then* does it make sense to think about extra perks for apprentices (if you choose). But a well-designed apprenticeship is already a high-quality program for the apprentice.

Bottom line: if you do not intentionally design your apprenticeship with operations and profitability in mind, your apprenticeship program becomes a cost center. And we all know what happens to overhead costs—they're the first programs to get cut. We don't do that here. It's a bad look for the business and bad for the apprentices.

In Section III, we'll look at the main aspects of designing your program, including curriculum (both hard and soft skills), mapping curriculum to competencies and requirements, assessing apprentices, organizing the coursework, and creating a classroom plan. We will then dive into how to integrate on-the-job training, set up a wage progression system, and effectively budget for your program. Finally, we'll cover strategies for recruiting apprentices, scheduling their training, and ensuring they stay on track. By the end of this section, you'll have a comprehensive roadmap to create, manage, and optimize a successful apprenticeship program from scratch.

Time to roll up our sleeves.

Create Some Free Social Capital

First, a brief detour. Social capital refers to the network of relationships and trust that individuals build through acts of kindness and mutual support. It's the byproduct of helping others without expectations, and it enriches both the giver and the community. In Adam Grant's book *Give and Take*, he cited a study that has shown for every $1 someone gives, they generate $3.74 in return.[12] Is there some sort of cosmic mutual fund that spits out returns? No, the reason this increase in income occurs is because the type of person who gives money is also the type of person who helps others, and in turn, they receive help for their own careers and endeavors. Call it God's grace, karmic deposits, or the universe conspiring for you.

I'd like to create an opportunity for you with this simple question: *would you help a stranger if it didn't cost you a penny but* you *never got credit for it?*

If so, I'd like to make an ask on behalf of someone out there who is just like you or like you were a few years ago: less experienced, wanting to grow their business and people, seeking information but unsure where to look . . . This is where you come in. The only way for us at Apprentix to accomplish our mission of helping businesses grow through the power of apprenticeships is, first, by reaching them.

Most people do, in fact, judge a book by its cover (and its reviews). If you have found this book valuable thus far, would you please take a brief moment right now to leave an honest review of the book and its contents? It will cost you zero dollars and less than sixty seconds.

---

[12] Adam Grant, *Give and Take: Why Helping Others Drives Our Success*, (Penguin Books, 2013) (Referencing UnitedHealth Group's "Doing Good is Good for You: 2013 Health and Volunteering Study").

Your review will help . . .

- One more business create an apprenticeship program
- One more person become an apprentice
- One more person teach the next generation
- One more life change for the better

All you have to do is take less than sixty seconds to leave a review.

If you're reading a physical copy of the book: Go to Amazon and scroll to the "Reviews" section. Look for "Review this product" and click on the "Write a customer review" button. On mobile, scroll to the bottom of the page to find the button to write a review.

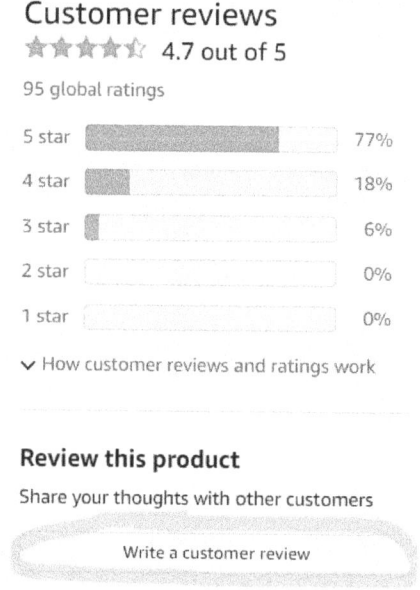

If you're reading this on Kindle or an e-reader: Scroll to the bottom of the book, then swipe up. It will automatically prompt a review.

If you're reading this on the Kindle app or an e-reader: Tap the three dots in the top right of your device, tap on "Before you go," and click the number of stars you'd rate the book, then leave a sentence or two about the book.

If you're listening to this on Audible: Hit the three dots at the top of your device, click "Rate & review," then leave a sentence or two about the book with a star rating.

PS: If there's something in particular that you've struggled with that you think someone else might struggle with too, please mention it in the review. When someone sees they're not alone, they feel more confident to learn.

PPS: Social capital maximizer—If you introduce something valuable to someone, they associate that value with you. If you'd like to create social capital with another business colleague, send this book their way.

Thank you from the bottom of my heart. Now, let's hop back in.

With gratitude,

Andy

Coursework Designer

Apprenticeship Occupations

First, let's talk about what jobs, a.k.a. occupations, you're going to apprentice. Start by looking at the business and saying, "What are our entry-level roles?" Then ask yourself, "Do these roles seem like ones that we would apprentice?" Maybe you have new-hire roles that makes sense for a project and that you could put into the apprenticeship program.

Another way to look at this is to ask, "Do I have a gap in a certain band of my workforce?" Maybe you have plenty of frontline workers, but the level above them is sparse. You may identify that second tier as the job to be apprenticed.

Ultimately, you're identifying the occupations you want to apprentice, and as I mentioned before, you don't want to have a proliferation of occupations being apprenticed. You want to keep the total number of occupations being apprenticed rather narrow. It's in your best interest to have fewer programs covering the greatest number of apprentices.

Once you've determined which occupations you want to apprentice, it's time to figure out what you'll teach them.

Coursework Design

Figuring out the right coursework for apprentices is a complex issue. Should you create it, buy it, or source it from somewhere else? We're going to tackle all these options.

Essentially, coursework design is about deciding what to teach so that your apprentices truly get it. You can design your own courses or purchase them. While managing this might seem daunting, there's a straightforward way to do it. We've done it successfully for hundreds of businesses, and though the process might seem counterintuitive, it's incredibly effective. Hang in there, because I'm going to show you exactly how it's done.

What's the Point of Apprentices Taking Classes?

We've already talked about the need for apprentices to take classes alongside their on-the-job training. This isn't just a formality; it's essential to combine classroom theory with practical experience. Without the theory, it's just job training, not a true apprenticeship.

The real value comes from understanding both what's supposed to happen (the theory) and what actually happens on the job (the hands-on application). This dual approach ensures that apprentices don't just perform tasks but truly understand the underlying principles, which enhances their ability to get it—comprehend the job, want it—be motivated to do it, and have the competency to execute it effectively.

Let's say somebody is out on the job. They're working on something and they're getting trained on a particular skill, but they don't know what it's supposed to look like. They don't know what's supposed to happen. All they know is what has happened. They don't necessarily have the background to say, "You know what? This isn't good enough. This should be better." And this affects the quality of your work, the quality of their output. That's why theory is so important. It helps them understand what's supposed to happen versus what they see actually happen.

The second reason is because when an apprentice is on the job and they don't have any classroom theory, they waste the time of higher-cost labor (i.e., highly skilled people). The apprentice's questions could have easily been answered through a low-cost avenue: coursework. The wasted time of the apprentice and the higher-skilled person is a cost to the business in lost productivity. It's a margin that you're losing and not just the cost of that person. Train an apprentice in the classroom and your costs are limited to the cost of instruction. Train an apprentice on the job and your costs are both the cost of the training and the opportunity cost of lost productivity.

It's also frustrating for the journeymen, of course, because they're thinking, "Why don't you know this stuff already?" The apprentices don't know it because they haven't been taught it. Is it the journeymen's job to teach that? No, it's an instructor's job to teach that theory. It's the journeymen's job to show them how. That's really where the difference is, but there's a great return on investment if you invest in coursework at the right cost structure so that you avoid wasting the time of somebody who's expensive.

How to Make Your Own Curriculum

Creating your own curriculum is a very scalable approach. Yes, there's going to be some investment upfront, but it's a high-value, low-cost approach. One of the ways businesses can be successful in their apprenticeship programs is by designing their own curriculums when possible. They also supplement it by buying other people's curriculums. I don't want to say one is better or worse, but I will say that the businesses that can deliver curriculums themselves at a low cost have much greater ROI potential than businesses that buy expensive coursework do.

First things first: You want to teach a person what they need to know to do that job at your company. Start with the end in mind and figure out what it is they need to know how to do. This is called a list of competencies. Come up with a list of competencies by either Googling or using ChatGPT. Search "list of competencies for [occupation name]."

Next, it's crucial to include both hard and soft skills in your curriculum. Hard skills, or technical skills, require specific training for job functions. Soft skills, or behavioral skills, are observable actions and behaviors. Essentially, hard skills involve doing specific tasks, while soft skills involve how one behaves and interacts in the workplace.

Example: Construction Laborer

Hard Skills

❏ Operate pumps or compressors
❏ Clean equipment or facilities
❏ Maintain construction tools or equipment

Soft Skills

❏ Attention to detail
❏ Problem-solving abilities
❏ Communication skills

Let's take a quick look at the example of a construction laborer. In the graphic, you can see a list of hard skills and a list of soft skills, and you can see the difference between them. In fact, if you have a time-based apprenticeship program, you'll have time allocated to the hard skills. But those soft skills... it's hard to say that if somebody's worked on communication skills for ten hours, they're now competent. It doesn't quite work that way. Those are more observational and behavioral in nature, and those would require evaluations.

> **Pro Tip: Use Apprentix to Automatically Generate Competencies for 57,000+ Occupations**
>
> Apprentix's database has over 57,000 occupations in it, and it's still growing! Just select the job title you're interested in apprenticing and Apprentix will automatically generate the competencies for that job, which are also approved for registering your apprenticeship.

Add What You Already Have

You can mine the information you already have for coursework. One of the ways you can do this is to look at existing internal documents. Ask yourself, "When a new hire starts, how do I currently train them on this? What do I already have in writing that I can use?" That's going to be the start of your curriculum.

- Start with the **company's information**. What documents do you already have on your company's founding story, its mission, vision, and values, and your products and services? Whatever you have already written down would be perfect fodder for a course.

- Add **policies**. Most businesses have HR policies. That's also a course. You need your apprentices to know the HR policies.

- Add **processes**. This includes training manuals and standard operating procedures. Anything that defines the work processes is also great coursework.

Take what you have and use those as assets—they are the start of the curriculum that you will begin to organize and add to as you take the next steps.

Write or Record What You Know

Then ask yourself, "What is it that I can teach that I don't already necessarily have written down?" You may decide to write down what you need to teach, or you may record videos of yourself talking and have the recordings transcribed. The recordings themselves could be videos, audio files, or both that make the information accessible for your apprentices.

Once you've exhausted what you already have in writing and what you'd like to teach, you may be left with a gap between what needs to be taught and how to teach it. That's where purchasing courses comes into play.

Where Can You Buy Hard-Skills Training?

Where you find hard-skills training depends on your industry and location. You can look for ready-made courses, train an in-house trainer, or search for resources. Registered apprenticeship programs may have access to accredited curriculums.

Look for Ready-Made Courses

Let's start with looking at industry associations. Industry associations have what's called content banks. A lot of them have a mission to educate the workforce, so they have created training programs or partnered with people who have created training programs that you might be able to access for free or at a low cost. You might also be able to find training programs for industry-specific occupations that have been created by your industry associations. I would absolutely check there and see what they've got.

Another option is to look at industry training centers. For example, in Denver, we have a couple of training centers focused on construction occupations where people can go. You can send your workers to these training centers as well. But you should, once again, contact your industry association and ask them what kind of training centers they mine. If this is a registered apprenticeship program, this is the perfect opportunity to ask your industry association, "Do you have an industry training program, whether it's online content or an in-person training provider who meets the DoL's requirements?"

When you look for these courses, here's what you should ask about:

- **Cost.** Number one, what's the cost? Pretty obvious.

- **Start date.** This is important because a start date means you have the time when this apprentice is going to start their coursework versus when they started their job as an apprentice. You don't have to start coursework on the first day of an apprentice's job. They can have done on-the-job learning and be tracking hours toward that and then begin their coursework. That's totally fine. Obviously, the longer they go without learning any classroom theory, the more difficult that will be. But it's certainly acceptable to do that. You just want to figure out what the start date is and then figure out whether you'll start a group of people, known as a cohort, together or whether you'll allow rolling admissions, and how that would work if there is a start date for these classes. Obviously, for on-demand online classes, that won't matter so much, but it's important to know the start date for in-person classes.

- **Duration.** The duration needs to fit the timing of the apprenticeship program. If the coursework itself is going to take a year and a half and you know the apprentice will be on a project for only a year, it's not a good idea to enroll them in a program where they're going to finish working without finishing their apprenticeship. That's important because the bulk of return doesn't come upfront on hiring the apprentice. The bulk of the return comes after they've been trained, so that could happen after three months, six months, or whatever it is. But all that productivity gain becomes profit margin, so you don't want to give up that profit margin.

This is relevant only if you're putting people on a project for a year and then your business model is that they are terminated because there won't necessarily be another project for them to work on. If you have projects where people are constantly rolling into the next one and rolling into the next ones, this doesn't really matter because they're going to have the duration on the job that works with the training program.

- **Curriculum**. What courses are they going to teach? Look at it from a competency standpoint and say, "Okay, does what the provider teaches line up with what I need the apprentices to know?"

Train the Trainer

Under this model, you purchase coursework to train somebody in-house who then trains apprentices. A common example of this is the training materials available from the National Center for Construction Education and Research (NCCER). The NCCER is an accredited body, and instructors must pass its course to become accredited NCCER instructors to then train others on NCCER coursework. Under the train-the-trainer model, you're paying for the training once, and then your business can train people.

There are a couple of things to point out here. One, obviously, is that you must choose an instructor. Two, you need a backup for that person in case they're out, or if they turn over, or if they just can't perform that duty for a while. Whatever the reason, you need a trained backup instructor.

Search for Resources

Where else can you buy hard-skills training? You can do something really simple: turn to Google or ChatGPT and search "list of trade-specific online platforms for [occupation]." For example, I can prompt ChatGPT with "Find a list of trade-specific online platforms to train a construction laborer" and then refine the search with "What about somebody local to this area?" It's important to search for local training providers because, for instance, community colleges can only train people locally. Well, you can ask about that too, but this is a great way for you to find different training and coursework resources.

Curriculum for Registered Programs

And sidebar, if you register your apprenticeship program, you could purchase a curriculum from a provider on the Eligible Training Provider List (ETPL) and receive public funding to subsidize some of the cost. Since every state has their own list of ETPLs, you're best off doing a search for "[state] Eligible Training Provider List."

This will likely produce a long list of organizations, many of which are businesses that provide education for their own apprentices in-house and are willing to sell you their training. These are known as employer-sponsored training providers. You'd have to abide by their rules, so even though this is an option, it's rarely done. Purchasing an employer-sponsored training provider's curriculum is most common among larger organizations and those in industries with a high demand for skilled labor, such as manufacturing, health care, and technology.

Now, I will warn you: If you've been told to contact a workforce development center to find an eligible training provider, know that their turnaround time and quality of response can be . . . let's just say the uncomfortable part out loud: It's the government. They don't exactly have service-level agreements (SLAs) they must meet.

Outsourced Training Providers with Labs

Labs are something that you might find with outsourced training providers in your area who not only provide classroom instruction but also have lab time or shop class time. This isn't the same as on-the-job training, but it does help you because more of the training is done at the education provider's site. An example of this here in Colorado is the Construction Industry Training Council of Colorado, which offers both classroom instruction and a lab component.

Pro Tip: Virtual Reality Training

Several companies are emerging to provide virtual reality training. I first learned about this from one of our customers who was in a remote part of Texas and couldn't access training locally. They went with a VR solution to supplement their in-house training, and it's worked well for them. The companies are likely to evolve and grow in this space, so I'd recommend you search for your industry or occupation and add "virtual reality training." Here is a provider I know of that has gained traction in this space: *Transfr VR: https://transfrinc.com*

Where Can You Buy Soft-Skills Training?

You can buy soft-skills training all over the internet (and some of it is free). I encourage you to do this because soft-skills training is a great way for apprentices to be trained even while they're in between tasks. For example, if they're working outside and it's raining and they've got some downtime, they can just pop open their phones and do these courses. Here are several popular resources:

- **LinkedIn Learning (free with a library card!)** acquired a company called lynda.com years ago, and I've been using this with my own apprentices for years and years and years. I've told many people about this too. LinkedIn Learning has experts who teach all kinds of soft skills. Currently, it costs something like $40 a month, but if your apprentice has a local library card or can and is willing to get a local library card, they can access LinkedIn Learning for free. And that's a heck of a deal because the library of courses there is unbelievable.

- **Coursera** has a huge catalog of expertly done yet inexpensive courses. And they run promotions on them all the time. You can even set up a business account so that you can purchase courses and license them out to apprentices or allow apprentices to complete courses as part of your business account, without having to share logins.

- **Udemy** features a wide range of courses on soft skills. You can find courses tailored to improving communication, leadership, and problem-solving skills. The advantage of Udemy is the breadth of courses available, suitable for different levels of expertise.

- **edX** hosts free courses from universities around the world. You can find courses on topics such as effective communication, teamwork, and leadership. These are often more academic in nature.

- **Skillshare** focuses on creative and interactive learning. Look for courses that enhance creativity, collaboration, and personal development, which are crucial soft skills in the workplace.

- **Khan Academy** is known for its educational courses. It offers resources on personal development and soft skills, though they are more limited in scope compared to others.

- **Alison** offers free online courses with a focus on workplace skills, including soft skills such as communication, leadership, and stress management.

Map Your Coursework to Competencies

Mapping coursework to competencies involves aligning your training materials with the specific skills and abilities your apprentices need to master. This process ensures that every element of your curriculum directly supports the development of the competencies required for their roles, making the training both relevant and effective.

Construction Laborer: Training Sources

Hard Skills	
Competency to be trained	*Training source*
Operate pumps or compressors	Training manuals
Clean equipment or facilities	SOP for cleaning equipment
Maintain construction tools or equipment	Nothing documented - train this on the job

Soft Skills	
Competency to be trained	*Training source*
Attention to detail	Udemy's "Attention to Details" course
Problem-solving abilities	LinkedIn's "Problem Solving" course
Communication skills	LinkedIn's "Learning Communications" course

Coming back to our construction laborer example, take your list of competencies and divide them into hard skills and soft skills. Now write down all the things you already have that you can use for training. You'll end up with a list of hard and soft skills, along with how you're going to train apprentices.

Delivery Mechanisms

Now, how do you deliver this information? If you have it written down, delivery will be simple—you're going to deliver it in writing. If you don't already have it written down but you have books or training manuals on this, use what you have. If you don't have anything in writing, you'll need to determine which delivery method you're going to use to get that information to apprentices. You can write it down or record yourself speaking—whatever you're more comfortable with, get the information out of your head and into a format for apprentices to consume. It doesn't need to be perfect. It doesn't need to be heavily edited. It just needs to convey the information you teach.

I will say, though, that engaging content will hold the attention of the apprentice longer. Do you remember having a boring teacher at school and nodding off all the time? The head nod—oh my gosh, that head nod. You want to prevent the head nod. You have to make it engaging. Try to inject some personality into it as opposed to just reading a script. But ultimately, the main thing is that you convey the information and that they learn it.

Create Assessments Like Quizzes or Tests

One of the best ways to ensure that learning is taking place is to create assessments or quizzes and be able to assess the apprentices on what they've just learned. This isn't too different from what schools do—they test students. So you want to create assessments as well.

You can create assessments in any format: in a Word document, in a Google form. If you're using Apprentix, we have a whole assessment section where you can create templated assessments and then assign them to any apprentices you want, as much as you want. You can store all the scores in there and share that data. You can use the function in all kinds of ways.

Also, assessments show exactly how each apprentice has performed and what they've learned, and they help you see their performance progress. If they haven't really understood a concept and then over time start to improve, you can see that they truly do seem to understand it. You want to be able to give assessments to ensure that the knowledge is embedded and not just have them read something and say, "Yeah, I get it." Maybe they get it, but maybe they don't. Assessments are an important intermission between each of the things that you want them to learn.

Putting It All Together: An Example Curriculum

So how do we look at assembling all of this? Here's an example. You can see we've divided up the company, the policies, the hard skills, and the soft skills. Underneath each one are all the training materials we already have or we're going to purchase. And after they're all slotted in, we've effectively got our curriculum. That's it.

Delivery Mechanisms: Construction Laborer

Company
- ❑ Mission, vision, and values
- ❑ Products and services

Policies
- ❑ HR
- ❑ Safety

Hard Skills
- ❑ Operate pumps or compressors
  - ❑ Training manuals
- ❑ Clean equipment or facilities
  - ❑ SOP for cleaning equipment
- ❑ Maintain construction tools or equipment
  - ❑ Nothing documented - need to train this on the job

Soft Skills
- ❑ Attention to detail
  - ❑ Udemy's "Attention to Details" course
- ❑ Problem-solving abilities
  - ❑ LinkedIn's "Problem Solving" course
- ❑ Communication skills
  - ❑ LinkedIn's "Learning Communications" course

Designing effective coursework for apprentices is key to the success of your apprenticeship program. Whether you create your own curriculum, purchase existing courses, or use a combination of both, the goal is to provide a balanced mix of theory and hands-on training. By making sure apprentices understand both the theoretical and practical aspects of their roles, you enhance their ability to perform tasks accurately and efficiently. Investing in quality coursework not only improves the learning experience for apprentices but also maximizes your business's return on investment by reducing training costs and boosting productivity.

Classroom Plan

A classroom plan differs from the coursework in that the classroom plan organizes all the courses by defining factors such as the number of classroom hours required, what information and materials are needed, and how you organize all the courses. Courses fit under the classroom plan, but it's hard to create the plan without knowing what courses you're going to offer first. That's why the classroom plan comes after the coursework. I'm going to dive into all these pieces here.

How Many Hours Should the Apprentice Take Classes?

In a registered apprenticeship program, the apprentice takes 144 hours of classes for every 2,000 hours of on-the-job training. That breaks down to roughly three hours a week on average. Some businesses choose to front load their training, or part of it, by having apprentices complete new-hire training and a large number of classroom hours before even stepping foot on the job. Other businesses spread the training out and ask the apprentice to take classes as part of their job or after work. It's up to you how you want to structure this to best suit your business.

If you are operating a registered apprenticeship program, there is a long-standing benchmark to use the 144 classroom hours for every 2,000 on-the-job hours. This is especially used in time-based apprenticeships with a fixed training duration (e.g., 3,000 hours).

In hybrid apprenticeships, where training duration is a range (e.g., 2,000 to 3,000 hours), there is potentially more flexibility in the number of classroom hours. You may have a minimum of 144 hours and a maximum of 216 hours. Federal and state institutions tend to calculate this differently. Some allow the lower end of the range, some require the upper end, and some allow you to enter the range.

If you run a competency-based program, there's no time requirement other than the apprenticeship needing to be a minimum of 2,000 hours, so your classes need to take only 144 hours because the program is competency based.

Pro Tip: Apprentix Automatically Calculates Classroom Hours

Once you select the occupation and training approach, Apprentix will show you how many hours that apprenticeship needs to last (the duration). Based on the duration and the training approach—whether time based, hybrid, or competency based—Apprentix will calculate the minimum number of classroom hours you need to fulfill and will require you to assign hours to each class so that the hours add up to the minimum requirement.

Once you've determined how many total hours of classes you need to have in your apprenticeship program, you must determine approximately how many hours each class will take. The reason is that apprentices must track their hours for each class to fulfill the apprenticeship requirements. Online and in-person classes have start and end times and add up to a certain number of hours, so it's easy to determine the number of hours per class. But what about the courses that are related to your company?

For example, how many hours will be spent talking about mission, vision, and values? You're not necessarily teaching a course on it. You might have materials for them to read. So how long does that take? This is where you get to use your best guesstimate. All that matters is that you have hours required against each course and that they total 144 hours per 2,000 hours of the job. You can make up however many hours that is.

Just remember that an apprentice is going to have to track their hours and allocate them to that particular course. If they've spent four hours in a class one day, they need to say, "I spent four hours on this class, or two hours on this one and two hours on that one." They will track, if there's a ten-hour requirement, the two hours they spent on it today, and the tracking will show that they've completed two hours of ten. If you're using Apprentix, apprentices can easily allocate those hours to the courses and to competencies.

Putting Together All the Information Required

To define the coursework itself, you need a few pieces of information:

- Course name

- Hours required per course

- Whether it's in person, online, or hybrid (a bit of both)

    o If it's in person, ask if there's a minimum number of absences.

    o If it's online, provide a link to the apprentice so that they know they can just click on it and it will take them directly where they need to go.

- Whether it's a required course and whether it's a core course. Some companies like to include optional courses for their apprentices, whereas other companies offer only required ones. If you do include optional courses, clearly show which courses are required and which are optional.

- Who the training provider is and who the instructor is—both show up on the transcript

- Any training materials that will be provided and the learning objectives of the course

By the way, all this information will automatically be added to the forms if you're registering a new apprenticeship program and you're using Apprentix. The information is included so that any state can accept it and see exactly what the coursework and classroom plan is going to be.

Organizing Coursework

Now that we've discussed creating coursework, it's time to think about how to organize it effectively. You need a system to manage all your courses, track progress, and ensure your apprentices are following the plan. One of the best ways to do this is by using a learning management system, but you can also use a shared drive if that works better for you. Let's explore how to set up your coursework in a way that's easy to manage and accessible for your apprentices.

Put the Coursework into a Learning Management System

A learning management system can help you organize your coursework. In simple terms, a learning management system is software or an app that helps you manage learning by facilitating everything from administration to assessments—and there are a thousand of them. The one we use internally is Trainual. (I don't have any affiliation with the company.) It's moderately priced and effective, and it organizes things in a logical manner for a business.

But honestly, learning management systems are a dime a dozen, and you can pick one that works for you. All you have to do is upload your content into it, and it will walk users through the training. They click on the relevant links and read or watch the content you provided. As they work their way through the courses, everything is marked completed. If you've created assessments, they can just take the assessments there.

Let's take a quick look at what it looks like if you add coursework to a learning management system. The graphic shows courses specific to our company, and you can see how the system breaks it down. The different screens represent the different tiers, if you will, and you can assign who has to take what course, who has completed courses, and so on.

Once an apprentice learns about our company, they move on to learning about our policies:

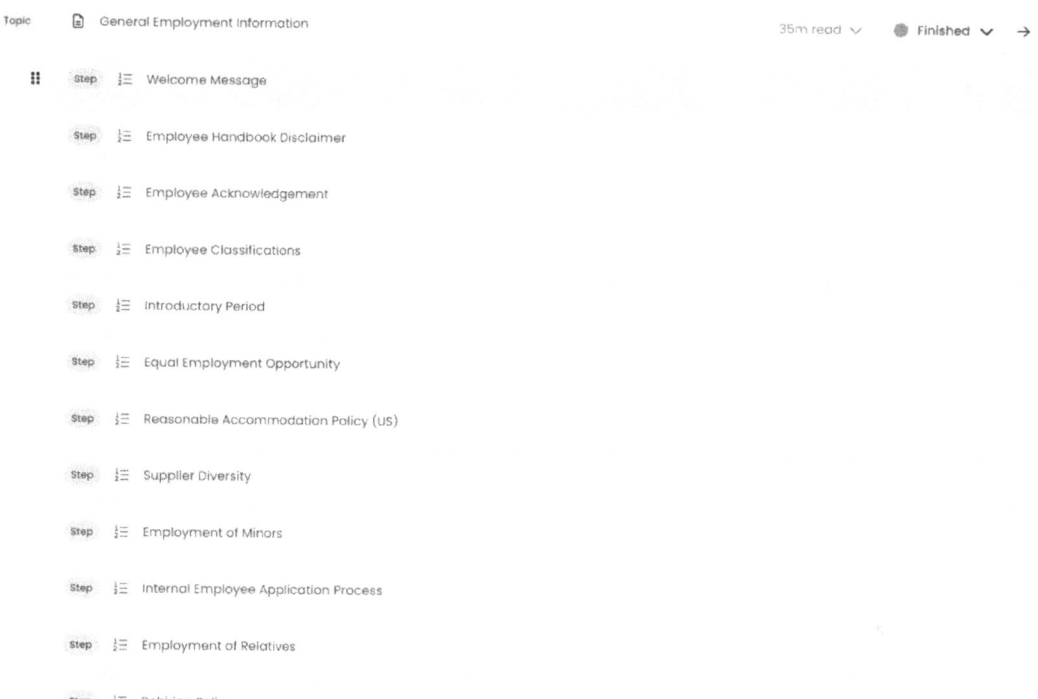

And finally, the apprentice is introduced to all the processes relevant to them:

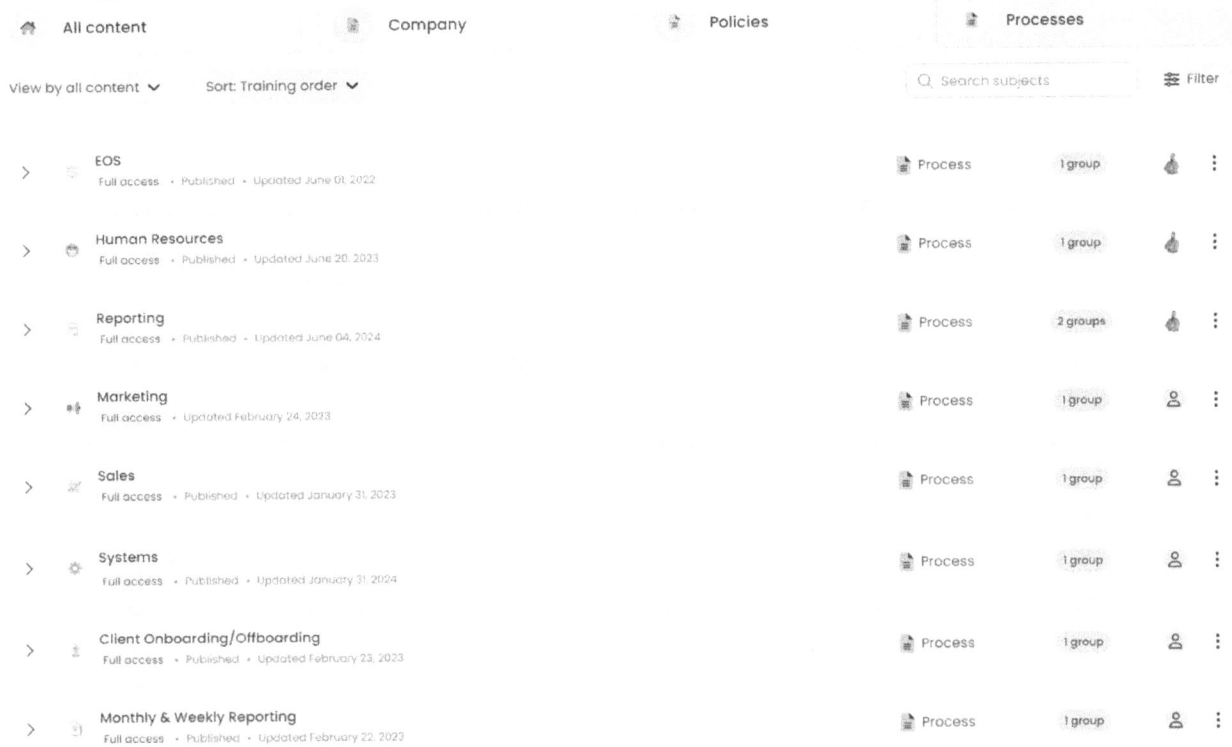

Or Heck, Just Use a Shared Drive

The other option is that you don't use a learning management system and that you put all your materials onto a shared drive. A shared drive is a space where teams can store, access, and search for files from any device. Examples of shared drives are Google Drive, Dropbox, and OneDrive. There's a good chance your company already has a shared drive set up that you can use.

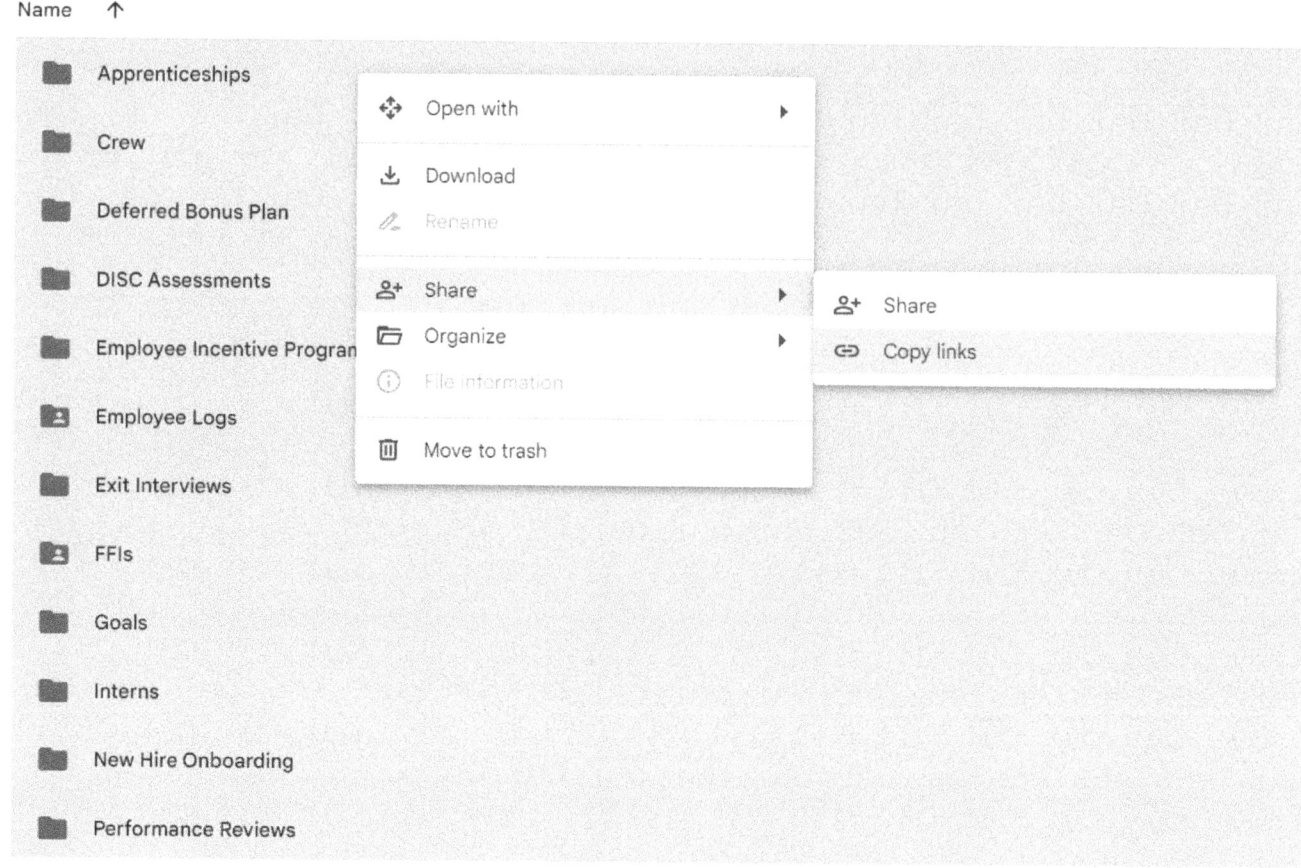

Example of a shared drive where you can copy the links and share them with apprentices. If you're using Apprentix, you can paste the link to each folder as a course in Apprentix.

Have the folders organized so that you can easily provide the name of each course and the corresponding link to the shared folder.

In Apprentix, you can add a list of all your courses and provide apprentices with links directly to those courses. I intentionally didn't build a learning management system into Apprentix. This was a strategic decision because a million of these systems are available already, and plenty of people have their own. If you have your own learning management system, use it in conjunction with Apprentix, and if you don't have one, you can get one or not.

It's Not That Hard—You Can Do It Yourself

Knowing how to create and purchase your own coursework will save you months of back and forth with federal or state apprenticeship agencies. Too often, businesses excited about starting an apprenticeship program get stuck in a frustrating cycle with their workforce development center or state apprenticeship representative, only to find that these entities lack the skills to develop or even properly source learning programs. The reality is that your business is best equipped to determine what the coursework should be. Government agencies can't give you all the answers or reveal others' methods—often because they don't know or because it's proprietary information. I've laid out where to get hard- and soft-skills training, develop your own, and where to buy it. This approach is the most effective and prevents the enthusiasm for your apprenticeship program from fading due to bureaucratic delays.

The issue isn't that creating coursework is hard—it's that the resources you're asking for coursework lack the expertise to create it for your business. They might provide generic links, but that's not enough. By following the breakdown I've given you, you can avoid wasting time and get the answers you need more efficiently. So take charge: use your existing materials, skills in speaking and writing, and ability to source courses to develop the coursework yourself.

Now that you've got a handle on organizing your coursework, it's time to look ahead to the next critical component: job training. We've covered how to create a cohesive classroom plan, set up your coursework in a learning management system or shared drive, and track progress effectively. With this foundation in place, you're ready to tackle the practical aspects of on-the-job training. In the next chapter, we'll dive into the Apprentix Job Training Converter, which helps align your existing work processes with your apprenticeship program. This approach ensures that your apprentices receive comprehensive, integrated training that supports both their development and your business goals. Let's move on and see how we can make your on-the-job training just as effective and structured as your classroom plan.

Job Training Converter

Once you have a handle on your classroom curriculum, it's time to put together your on-the-job training program. In this chapter, I'm going to walk you through the Apprentix Job Training Converter, which will help you align your existing work processes with your apprenticeship program. Lastly, we'll look at some supplemental information that you can use to enhance your on-the-job training program should you choose to do so.

The Goal

Let's start with the goal of the Job Training Converter. What is the Job Training Converter? I'll explain why we've come up with this process and this framework to enhance the success of apprenticeship programs.

A mistake many companies make when they start apprenticeship programs is that they think they must create an entirely new program around their apprenticeships. That means they look at everything from scratch. What should an apprentice be learning? What is it that they need to do on the job? They create a whole program that operates independently of their business. As a result, the program and company are disjointed. In fact, I've even seen companies that treat their apprentices as though they're not employees, and that's not really the case. Apprentices are employees, and they should be completely integrated into the work you already do.

The Job Training Converter framework is simply this: it helps you take your existing work processes and turn them into a job training component of an apprenticeship program as opposed to creating a brand-new job training process from scratch that doesn't match or integrate with the work you're doing. This is a big differentiator between apprenticeship programs that work and ones that fail.

I'm going to walk you through this step by step. As I mentioned, the goal here is for you to take what you currently do and map it into an on-the-job training plan.

Start with Your Competencies List

Planning your on-the-job training starts with the competencies list we've already talked about.

The Goal

Take your existing training plan + workload and write them as competencies.

Description of Workload	Competencies
Hard Skills	**Hard Skills**
❑ Use the pump ➝	❑ Operate pumps or compressors
❑ Clean stuff up ➝	❑ Clean equipment or facilities
❑ Keep your tools in working order ➝	❑ Maintain construction tools
Soft Skills	**Soft Skills**
❑ Pay attention to the little things ➝	❑ Attention to detail
❑ Think about how to solve it ➝	❑ Problem-solving abilities
❑ Know when and how to say it ➝	❑ Communication skills

In the column on the left, the skills are described informally—in the way a business might talk about them or perhaps have even written about them. They might be a little fluffy, but they describe the concept. In the column on the right, they're written as formal competencies.

To turn your informal descriptions into competencies, simply match the informal descriptions to a list of formal competencies. If you're using Apprentix, you can access more than 57,000 job titles and occupations on the platform. You're almost guaranteed to find the relevant job title on there—and a job training plan already built out for you. You don't have to do anything but review it. If you like it, edit it, change it, whatever you want, but it is already prebuilt for you on the platform.

Map Your Existing Processes and Assign Trainers to Topics

To map the process, take your list of competencies and assign a trainer to each one. That becomes the workload. Somebody is going to teach each competency. You'll start to see that you already have a lot of on-the-job training. It might simply be that you haven't formalized the process as we're doing here. By formalizing your informal processes, you're not changing the work—you're translating the work that's being done into a list of competencies and then into language that the apprentice will understand. The apprentice will be able to say, "I need to know how to do this. I need to demonstrate that I'm good at doing this."

Competencies for Registered Programs

When you're registering your apprenticeship program, translating your existing workload into a list of competencies is crucial. This list is what the registration agency will review to ensure your program meets the necessary standards. Whether you're working with the Office of Apprenticeship (OA) or the State Apprenticeship Agency (SAA), they'll want to see that your competencies align with the job you're describing. This is the language they understand and will use to determine if your program matches the occupational standards.

Ensuring that the apprenticeship program meets these occupational standards is key. It involves outlining all the work that needs to be done as specific competencies and making sure those competencies align with the occupation. These are the standards your program will be judged against, so getting this right is essential for successful registration and compliance.

Future-Proof by Identifying Additional Skills Needed

The next step to take is to future-proof your apprenticeship program. It's crucial to not only focus on the skills your apprentices need right now but also to anticipate the skills they'll need in the future. For example, let's say you're a construction company and you're planning to implement a new building technology next year. You should write these upcoming skills into your competency plan now.

Take the example of a craft laborer. Currently, they might be proficient in using traditional tools and materials. However, if you know that your company is transitioning to more eco-friendly building methods, you need to start training your apprentices on these new techniques today. This way, when the new technology rolls out, your team is already prepared.

Another important aspect of future-proofing is identifying skill gaps. If you're trying to upskill someone into a higher position, which is essentially what an apprenticeship is all about, you need to identify what skills they're currently lacking. For instance, let's say you have plenty of frontline craft laborers but not enough foremen. You need to determine what skills your laborers lack to move up to foremen positions.

Look at these gaps and think about how you can train your team on the job to fill them. For instance, if leadership skills are lacking among your craft laborers, you could develop a training module focused on leadership and team management. By doing this, you're not only closing the skill gaps but also preparing your employees for promotion, ensuring you have the necessary talent to fill critical positions in your business.

Once you've mapped out what your business already does and translated that into a list of competencies for your apprentices, the next step is deciding how to approach the training. As we discussed in the curriculum section, you have three main options: a time-based, competency-based, or hybrid approach. Let's dive into each of these in more detail.

Training Approaches

When it comes to training approaches, you need to consider how you'll judge completion (time, competency, or a hybrid of those), how long your program will last, and how you'll evaluate your program. First, we'll explore completion requirements, or how your apprentices know they've completed the training. I'll walk you through the three options—the time-based, competency-based, and hybrid approaches.

Time-Based Approach

A time-based approach means that the apprenticeship in its entirety is all based on time. The apprentice needs to complete this many hours of this, this many hours of that, this many hours of this, and so on. That applies both to coursework and on-the-job training.

If you say, "This person needs to know how to hang drywall, and that's going to take fifty hours," the minute they've completed the fiftieth hour and it's been approved by their supervisor, that competency is marked as complete and they are marked as proficient in that competency. But is that true? It depends on the competency and on the company's training approach, but if you follow a time-based approach, you're saying that the only requirement to demonstrate competency is that the apprentice has done the time.

Some people would look at this and argue that that's not appropriate for their business or for that occupation. For them, the competency-based approach would be more suitable.

Competency-Based Approach

The competency-based approach means it doesn't matter how much time an apprentice has spent on a competency. Someone must have observed and evaluated the apprentice and said that they are in fact proficient in this competency, that they are capable of doing the job or using the skill.

Competency-based approaches do still have a minimum two-thousand-hour requirement. Don't think that somebody can just do a competency-based apprenticeship in less than two thousand hours if it's a registered apprenticeship. If your apprenticeship program isn't registered, I strongly encourage you to consider a competency-based apprenticeship, because what you want from a business perspective is people to learn the competencies and the skills as fast as possible so that they can generate as much return for you as possible. It's in your best interest to make apprenticeships as short as possible.

Some people might also look at this and say, "Well, I'm not really sure. Sometimes it might be time. Sometimes it might be evaluation." Fine, that's called a hybrid approach.

Hybrid Approach

The hybrid approach is useful when you want to require an apprentice to work a minimum number of hours on a competency and then evaluate whether they can do it or not. If the apprentice isn't proficient yet, you don't sign off on the competency until you observe that they can perform the actual work. However, there is also a maximum number of hours on a hybrid plan to ensure the apprentice isn't working more hours than needed simply because they haven't been evaluated yet.

Hybrid apprenticeships are also useful if you want to have a mix of time- and competency-based skills. Each competency can be categorized as time or competency based. You can have a list of twenty or two hundred competencies and say, "Competency number one is time based, competency number two is behavior based," and so on.

A word of caution: a hybrid approach provides the most flexibility, but you need to make clear to apprentices that even when they've satisfied the time requirement, they will still need to pass a behavioral evaluation before they will be signed off as being proficient in that skill.

Choosing a Training Approach

How do you determine which competencies are suitable for a time- or competency-based approach? From an apprentice's standpoint, and maybe even a supervisor's standpoint, I encourage you to think through how the determination of competency will be made. If somebody says, "Look, I know they spent twenty hours on this skill, but they still suck," do you want them to be marked proficient based on time and to move on? If not, a competency-based or hybrid approach is the better option.

The competency-based approach is probably the most practical for most jobs, but I recognize that in several occupations, especially in the trades, competencies have been time based and continue to be that way. In that case, consider a hybrid training approach. Ultimately, these are the conversations you want to have either within yourself or with your team.

In Apprentix, when you mark a skill as "technical" (a.k.a. time based), you must also enter the hours required. Hours can be tracked against the skill since it's time based. You can also mark a skill as "behavioral" (a.k.a. competency based), and hours will not be required. And apprentices can request behavioral competency evaluations because they obviously can't evaluate themselves. The request is routed to their supervisor, who performs the evaluation. Alternatively, the supervisor can simply do the evaluation without being prompted. That apprentice is evaluated on whether they're "not in training, "in training," or "proficient." One of the core features of Apprentix is to be able to do all that tracking on the platform.

Modification Rule (Registered Programs)

If you are providing a registered apprenticeship program, how much can you modify the competencies to fit your own business? According to the modification rule, apprenticeable occupations have defined lists of competencies (all that data is available in Apprentix), and you're allowed to modify only 25 percent of the established on-the-job training plan.

Here's the thing: Who checks that, and how do they measure 25 percent? Is it 25 percent in characters that can be edited? Is it sentences that can be edited? Is it full competencies? If you modify a word, is that considered an edit? The rule doesn't include any language clarifying what 25 percent means, and I can assure you there's no one doing a side-by-side comparison and then calculating the difference in the total number of characters that have been changed. There's just no real way to enforce this other than through spot checks. It's really an intention rule. The intent is to try not to change it too much because the organization is sold on this idea that if you're doing this job, this is what you should know how to do. But if you change it until it's unrecognizable, they're going to have a hard time with that.

That's basically the point—know that when you're generating an on-the-job plan, especially if you're generating one right out of Apprentix, it will spit the whole plan out for you. How much you modify that is up to you. No one is really going to be able to spot check this 25 percent rule, but know that the intention is to keep it somewhat intact.

I'll give you an example. Let's say the state develops an on-the-job training plan for a craft laborer and includes a competency called General Construction Skills with an allocation of five hundred hours. This summary might sound comprehensive, but when you break it down, there's no practical way to track time or evaluate performance based on that vague description.

To make it more practical, we need to specify what "General Construction Skills" entails. For instance, under this broad category, we might break it down into specific tasks, such as framing and installation (200 hours), basic electrical work (150 hours), and concrete mixing and pouring (150 hours). Each of these tasks includes detailed subcompetencies, such as reading blueprints for framing, safely wiring electrical outlets, and properly mixing concrete to required specifications.

By breaking it down this way, you can clearly track hours and evaluate performance on specific skills, rather than on a vague, all-encompassing competency. This detailed approach not only makes it easier for you to manage the apprenticeship but also ensures that apprentices are gaining the precise skills needed for the job. When you submit this detailed plan to the state, they'll appreciate the thoroughness and practical application of your training program.

I will also tell you that when I see what states put together for on-the-job training plans versus what's practical for practitioners, the difference is night and day. The state might summarize competencies to make the paperwork easy, but when you go into practice, you cannot operate that way.

I encourage you to not take what the state gives you but rather generate your plan out of Apprentix. Get the full list of competencies, use that, and submit it to the state.

The state will be thrilled. They're not going to say no to that. They love the fact that you know what you're doing. You will operate the apprenticeship by defining those competencies well.

Duration

Now let's talk a little bit more about the duration. We did mention how there's a duration for time-based occupations. For each apprenticeable occupation, the DoL has set how long each of those apprenticeships should be in terms of time. For example, for electricians, it's eight thousand hours. You can't modify it because you believe you can train an apprentice in four thousand hours. If you create a competency-based program, you might be able to do that, but then you also must make sure that the state approves the program if you're going to go register it.

If you're using a hybrid approach, it's a defined range of hours. Again, the information is listed in Apprentix, so it's super easy for you. If you said, "I want to do a time-based program," it'll say, "This is going to be eight thousand hours. Do you approve?" If you say, "I want to do a hybrid program," it'll say, "This is six thousand to eight thousand hours. Do you approve?" Whatever it is, Apprentix contains all the definitions of terms so that you know upfront what you're signing up for.

Be careful that you don't sign up for the wrong training approach and you don't realize how long you're signing up to do it. The other thing you want to look at when it comes to duration is to structure the term of the apprenticeship so that it works within whatever project you're working on. I'll give you an example. Let's say that you've got somebody working on a four-year apprenticeship program and they're on a project for two years. If they're going to rotate into another project after those two years, great—they can complete their apprenticeship program if their rotation into the next project aligns with what the work would be on the apprenticeship. If they go from doing one job for two years to a completely different job in two years, but they're training on job number one for four years, it's a mismatch. You want to look at the training approach and the duration specifically to match what you anticipate happening with that person.

The other thing to remember is that if you are working on a public project that requires apprenticeships, there's likely a requirement on the total number of labor hours that need to be performed by an apprentice. If you're doing this rotation, again, make sure that you're looking at the total number of hours the apprentice will work and will attend class. If they're rotating off this project and going to another project, can you still satisfy the hours that are required for your labor force to be apprentices?

By breaking down competencies into specific, trackable tasks, you can create a detailed and practical on-the-job training plan that aligns with state requirements and ensures your apprentices gain the precise skills needed for the job. This approach not only meets compliance standards but also enhances the effectiveness of your training program, making it easier to manage and more beneficial for your apprentices. When you submit this well-defined plan to the state, they'll appreciate the thoroughness and practical application, setting up your apprenticeship program for success.

Probationary Period (Registered Programs)

What exactly is a probationary period? A probationary period allows the business and apprentice to decide whether they want to continue the apprenticeship program. If one of the parties decides not to continue, the apprenticeship program can be terminated. The individual can remain an employee, but they'll no longer be an apprentice. That's important to note.

The probationary period must be defined a certain way for registered apprenticeship programs. It's either one year or up to 25 percent of the program's duration, whichever is shorter. For a two-year apprenticeship program, 25 percent is six months, so you can't do a one-year probationary period. For a four-year program, you could do a one-year probationary period, but you could also shorten it to nine months. Just remember, it's whichever is shorter—so it's one year, or up to 25 percent of the program's duration.

Why Is a Probationary Period Needed If Employment Is At Will?

If you're not operating a registered apprenticeship program, you can avoid all of this because you have an at-will employment agreement. The reason there's a probationary period specifically for apprenticeships isn't necessarily employment law. It has more to do with compliance reporting.

When a company has a registered apprenticeship program, it must report data that shows how successful it's been in graduating apprentices. If it terminates an apprentice during the probationary period, that apprentice doesn't count against its data. The apprentice doesn't show as somebody who was enrolled and who should have completed the program but didn't. That person is then basically eliminated from the data and doesn't count as a strike against the business. But if an apprentice is dismissed after the probationary period, the sponsor's data shows a zero out of one completion. So if that person doesn't finish and they made it past the probationary period, it's going to show up on the compliance records of the business, and it counts as a strike against the business for not having a good completion rate.

Why does this matter? Over time, the quality of an apprenticeship program is rated, in part, by the completion rate. If you're graduating 80 percent of your apprentices and a competitor is graduating only 30 percent of its apprentices, you would be more likely to be awarded the business because you're demonstrating a more reliable apprenticeship program.

I have heard that some states will suspend you from being able to bid on certain projects for a few years if the graduation rate of your program falls below 30 percent. Find out whether your state has this rule and whether it applies to work you're bidding on!

Another reason you might consider having a probationary period, even if you have at-will employment, is if your apprenticeship agreement includes specific reasons for termination. If you need to terminate someone for reasons not covered in the agreement, the probationary period gives you the flexibility to do that. It's a safety net that allows you to part ways without breaching the terms of the agreement. Plus, some regions have different laws for apprenticeship probationary periods than regular at-will employment, so it's worth checking your state's rules to make sure you're covered.

Creating an effective on-the-job training program is all about integrating your existing work processes into the apprenticeship framework. We've explored how to start with a list of competencies, map these competencies to trainers, and ensure they meet the standards required for registered programs. By breaking down broad competencies into specific, trackable tasks, you create a detailed and practical training plan. This not only meets compliance standards but also ensures your apprentices gain the precise skills they need for their roles. By organizing your training plan this way and using tools like Apprentix, you ensure that your apprenticeship program is not only compliant but also highly effective and practical for your apprentices and your business.

Gathering feedback from your team helps refine this plan, making it even more effective and practical. When you submit this thorough, well-defined plan to the state, you'll not only meet regulatory requirements but also set your apprenticeship program up for success.

Get Feedback

Once you have your whole list of competencies written out and developed, you might have edited some parts or added your own touches. Now it's crucial to get feedback from others within your company.

I've seen customers who use Apprentix do this well. Someone responsible for developing the on-the-job training sends the plan to the people who will be doing the training, such as the journey workers or managers. They ask, "Hey, would you mind taking a quick look at this? Do a sniff test and see if I missed anything they need to learn or if there's anything here that you really can't or shouldn't teach on the job. Maybe there's something that could be taught in a classroom instead."

Gathering this kind of feedback is invaluable. It helps ensure that the training plan is comprehensive, practical, and aligned with the realities of the job. Once you have their input, you can make the necessary modifications to your training plan.

Putting It All Together

What pieces of information do you need to have so that everything is compiled neatly and organized? If you're going to register, what kinds of information do you need to convey to the state agencies so that they understand exactly what your on-the-job training plan is?

First, you're going to look at the list of competencies and group the ones that make sense to go together into what's called a work process or a job function. Think of it like this: In tier one is the job function or work process, which is the overall process apprentices learning. Under that, you have the specific competencies they need to be competent in.

For example, let's say you have a job function called "Carpentry Work." Under this job function, you might have competencies like "Reading Blueprints" (150 hours), "Cutting and Shaping Materials" (200 hours), and "Assembling Structures" (250 hours). This grouping is useful for registering your apprenticeships because it provides a clear structure that both the apprentice and the state agency can understand. The apprentice can see "I've been working on Carpentry Work. What specific skills have I learned under that?" It aligns with how their mind works and how they track their progress.

Apprentix is set up according to this two-tier structure. You can easily group competencies together, and it makes sense. I encourage you to have the job function at the highest level, with competencies listed underneath.

Next, for each competency, you need to provide a description and define whether it's technical (requiring hours) or behavioral (evaluated based on performance). For example, "Reading Blueprints" might be technical, requiring 150 hours of training, while "Assembling Structures" could be behavioral, evaluated by observing the apprentice's proficiency.

Additionally, you need to specify if the training is online, in person, or a hybrid approach and categorize the competencies by year or semester—for instance, "Year One: Basic Carpentry Skills" and "Year Two: Advanced Carpentry Skills." In Apprentix, you can categorize these easily so that apprentices know exactly what they need to learn and when. This isn't necessary for the filing if you're going to register, but it is useful when organizing this information for an apprentice to check off and for the supervisor to know what work to assign.

Pro Tip: Use Apprentix for Time Tracking and Competency Evaluations

Payroll systems track the number of hours your apprentice works. However, apprenticeship programs require you to track the amount of time an apprentice worked **on each competency**. Apprentix does that for you.

Apprentix also allows you to observe an apprentice performing a task so that you can rate how competent they are in that competency. This is the step that all learning management systems miss: they test only knowledge, not competency. So if an apprentice has completed the technical hours for "Reading Blueprints," you can then observe and evaluate their actual ability to read and interpret blueprints on the job.

Wage Bump Builder

In this chapter, we're going to dive into building wage bumps (or increases), a unique feature of apprenticeships. Wage bumps can occur at the end of the apprenticeship program or somewhere in the middle. We'll discuss why these increases are important, how to define them, and how to implement them, especially if you're running a registered apprenticeship program, which requires at least one wage increase during the program.

First, I'll provide some context and background. Then, we'll get into the specifics of wage increases and discuss probationary periods, a unique aspect of registered apprenticeships that might be worth considering even if you don't have a registered program.

A wage increase means that while the apprentice is in their program, they get at least one raise before they complete it. This can be triggered by several factors: the total number of hours worked, achieving certain competencies, completing courses, or earning interim credentials.

For registered apprenticeship programs, a wage increase is mandatory, but even if you're not running a registered program, there are benefits to consider. By giving apprentices a wage increase as they learn and become more productive, you're showing them that their hard work and new skills are valued. This helps keep apprentices motivated, as they see a clear connection between their efforts and their earnings. Imagine the situation from an apprentice's perspective—they start as low-cost labor and naturally wonder, "When will I make more money?" By providing wage increases tied to their achievements, you're giving them tangible rewards for their progress. This motivates them to continue improving and contributes to a more engaged and productive workforce.

Three Main Elements for a Wage Increase

1. **Starting wage.** This is the wage the apprentice starts with. You can set this at the program level, ensuring that all apprentices start at least at the program's starting wage, which must meet state and city minimum wage requirements. While the starting wage can vary for different apprentices, it must always meet or exceed this baseline.

2. **Completion wage.** This is the wage the apprentice earns upon completing the program. Known as the journey worker's wage, it reflects their new role and responsibilities. In Apprentix, you can set both starting and completion wages at the apprenticeship level and then modify them for each apprentice.

3. **Wage increases.** These can be triggered for reasons such as time logged, course completion, or competencies achieved. Wage increases can be a percentage (e.g., 5 percent) or a specific dollar amount (e.g., $1 an hour).

Setting Up Wage Increases

There are two main ways to structure wage increases, especially for registered apprenticeships:

1. **Incremental increase.** Start with the initial wage (e.g., $15 an hour) and provide specific increases (e.g., $1 an hour after 2,000 hours or 5 percent after achieving a competency). The total increases don't need to add up to the completion wage; the apprentice might jump from $16 an hour to $20 an hour upon completion.

2. **Discount off completion wage.** Start with the completion wage (e.g., $20 an hour) and discount it for different milestones (e.g., 70 percent of $20 an hour for the first 1,000 hours, 75 percent for the next 1,000 hours, etc.). While this

approach is more common in registered apprenticeships, it requires translating percentages into actual dollar amounts for payroll.

Remember, regardless of the method, you'll need to convert these percentages or milestones into real dollars.

Dollar or percent decrease from completion wage

Completion wage = $20 per hour

Period	Hours	Wage (% of completion wage)	Wage Amount ($)
1	1,000	70%	$14
2	1,000	75%	$15
3	1,000	80%	$16
4	1,000	85%	$17

Note: Ultimately, you still need to translate this into actual dollars for each individual.

Now that we've covered the basics of wage bumps, let's move on to setting specific wages. We'll look at starting and completion wages and any increases along the way, including considerations for prevailing wages and wage evaluations.

Wage Progressions: What to Pay?

Wage progressions are crucial for your apprenticeship program. This is the system of giving your apprentices scheduled pay raises as they advance through their training. Think of it as a built-in reward system that keeps your apprentices motivated and ensures they see the value in sticking with your program.

Why does this matter? Imagine being an apprentice and knowing that with each new skill you master, your paycheck gets a little bigger. It's a tangible way of saying,

"Hey, we appreciate your hard work and dedication." It also helps retain talent because apprentices see a clear path to higher earnings without having to leave for a better-paying job elsewhere.

For example, let's say you have an apprentice starting at $15 an hour. As they hit specific milestones in their training—maybe mastering a new technique or completing a critical project—they get a raise. By the time they finish the program, they might be earning $20 an hour. This wage bump isn't just good for them; it's good for you too. You're investing in their growth, and in return, they're more likely to stay loyal and productive.

Wage progression also sets clear expectations. Your apprentices know what they need to do to earn those raises, which can boost their engagement and performance. It's not just about money—it's about creating a structured path for their career development within your company.

So when you're designing your apprenticeship program, think about how you can implement a wage progression system that rewards skill acquisition and hard work. It's a win-win for everyone involved.

Identify Starting Wage

The first question is "What do I pay an apprentice?" You need to identify the starting wage. How do you do that? Look at what you pay new hires already. A new hire in the occupation that will be apprenticed is the same thing as an apprentice, other than they're not enrolled in the apprenticeship program. What do you pay those people now? That's the starting point, but then you need to cross-reference it with some data, and then you'll be able to see where exactly you should start the apprentice. The data you need can be found on O*NET OnLine, a website funded by the DoL: https://www.onetonline.org.

The O*NET database includes information on skills, abilities, knowledge, work activities, and interests associated with occupations. Simply search for the relevant occupation.

Wage Progressions: What to Pay

#1 Identify Starting Wage

1. What do you pay your new hires?

2. Go to OnetOnline.org > search occupation

3. Scroll to "Wages & Employment Trends"

4. Select your State or Zip and click Go

Wages & Employment Trends

Median wages (2022)	$19.59 hourly, $40,750 annual
State wages	Colorado
Local wages	ZIP Code
Employment (2022)	1,413,600 employees
Projected growth (2022-2032)	Average (2% to 4%)
Projected job openings (2022-2032)	129,400
State trends	Select a State
Top industries (2022)	Construction

Colorado Wages
47-2061.00 - Construction Laborers · Bright Outlook

Wages for state: Colorado

Wages near ZIP Code:

Annual Wages   Hourly Wages

4. Select "Hourly Wages" tab

5. Use the low end and start with that (no one will penalize you for paying more!)

*Wages & Employment Screenshots from O*NET OnLine*

Let's say you're looking for a craft laborer. Type "craft laborer" into the search bar, and you'll get a list of occupations that closely or exactly match your search. Scroll to find the job you want, click on the link, and then scroll down to the "Wages & Employment Trends" section. Select your state or type in your zip code and click Go.

From there, select the Hourly Wages tab above the distribution graph or curve. Look at the low end and start with that. If you decide to pay an apprentice more than the low end that you start them with on paper, no one's going to be mad at you. If they're starting at $15 an hour and the first wage increase is to $17 an hour and they complete at $20 an hour, but you pay them $19 an hour from the beginning, you never have to implement the wage increase because their wage was already increased. You do have to pay them the $20 an hour once they've completed the program. That's important to understand.

But to identify a starting wage, start with the low end of the distribution curve. Compare that rate to what you pay the new hires to find a happy medium and choose the starting wage for the apprentice.

Identify Completion Wage

To identify the completion wage, start by looking at your own payroll to see what you pay a journey worker, or the next level up, for the job that's being apprenticed.

Wage Progressions: What to Pay

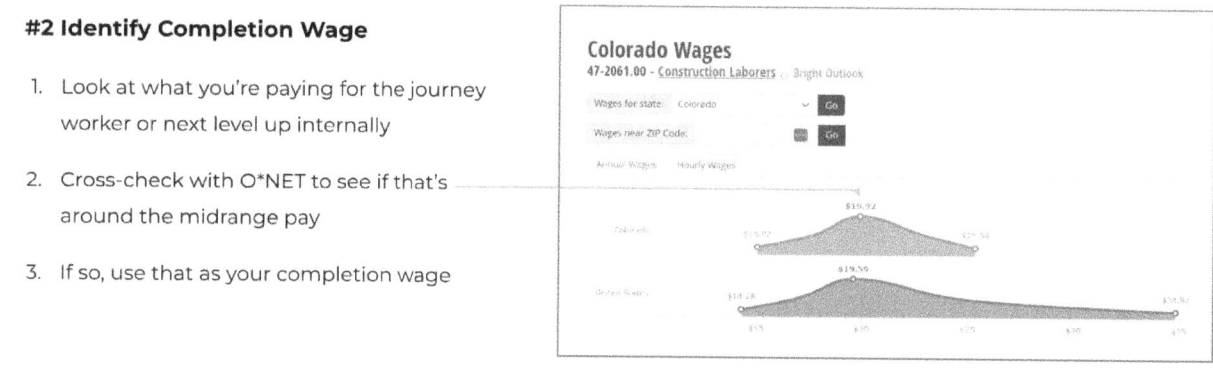

*Wages Screenshot from O*NET OnLine*

Go back to O*NET and, on the same graph you used in the previous step, check the midrange pay for that occupation. The midrange wage shows the wages for people who have completed their apprenticeships. Compare that to what you're paying somebody at that level now and you'll find the completion range.

Identify Wage Increase

A simple wage increase would be right down the middle of the starting and completion rates, and you could set the middle point at halfway through the program. You can simply pick a competency that's midway through the completion time of the apprenticeship program or just use the midway point of your apprenticeship program if it's time based. However, I encourage you to think about how you can dangle a carrot along the way to keep the apprentice moving on their own.

To keep apprentices motivated, you can divide the time between the start and end of the apprenticeship into multiple periods. For example, for a two-year program, you might divide the program into one-year periods or even six-month periods. For a four-year program, you'll want a raise at least once a year. Most employees expect an annual performance-based raise, so a raise once a year is sensible. Could you offer raises more frequently? Sure, you absolutely can, but you do want to keep dangling a carrot so that they keep moving and feel like there's an incentive for them to keep moving.

Wage Progressions: What to Pay

#3 Identify Wage Increase(s)

1. Come up with at least 1 wage increase

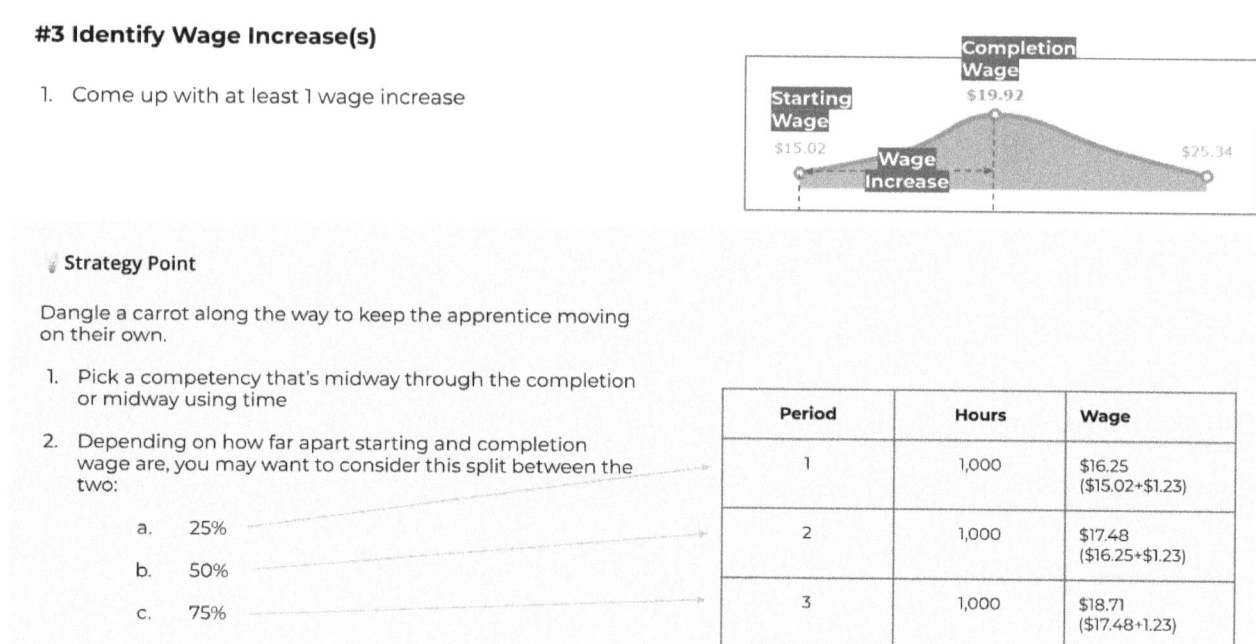

⚡ **Strategy Point**

Dangle a carrot along the way to keep the apprentice moving on their own.

1. Pick a competency that's midway through the completion or midway using time

2. Depending on how far apart starting and completion wage are, you may want to consider this split between the two:

    a.   25%

    b.   50%

    c.   75%

Period	Hours	Wage
1	1,000	$16.25 ($15.02+$1.23)
2	1,000	$17.48 ($16.25+$1.23)
3	1,000	$18.71 ($17.48+1.23)

Prevailing Wage

Prevailing wage is another important concept for your apprenticeship program. This term might sound a bit technical, but it's straightforward once you break it down.

So what is the prevailing wage? Simply put, it's the average wage paid to workers in a specific region for a particular job. Think of it as the going rate or market standard for certain types of work in your area. This rate is often determined by government agencies and is used to ensure that workers are paid fairly, especially on public projects.

Imagine you're running an apprenticeship program in construction. If the prevailing wage for a carpenter in your area is $25 an hour, that's the baseline you need to meet or exceed when paying your apprentices. It ensures that wages are competitive and fair, preventing undercutting and promoting quality workmanship.

Why does this matter for your apprenticeship program? If your apprentices are working on government-funded projects, you're usually required to pay them the prevailing wage. It's about compliance and ensuring that all workers, including apprentices, are compensated fairly, according to the standards of the industry and region. Paying the prevailing wage also helps attract top talent to your program. When apprentices know they're being paid what's standard for their role, they'll be more likely to join and stay in your program. It's a win for your recruitment efforts and helps maintain a high standard of work.

When setting up your apprenticeship program, make sure you understand and adhere to the prevailing wage requirements in your area. It's not just about following the rules—it's about valuing your apprentices and ensuring they're paid fairly for their hard work.

Now, a quick side note: If you are working on a public project with Davis–Bacon Act requirements, you need to pay prevailing wages. If this doesn't apply to you, feel free to skip ahead. But for those who do need to comply, here's a shortcut.

First, go to SAM.gov to find the prevailing wage for the occupation and location in your state.

Wage Progressions: What to Pay

#4 Prevailing Wage

1. For projects subject to prevailing wage requirements such as the Inflation Reduction Act, you must use the prevailing wage for an occupation to determine the completion rate.

2. You would then apply your discount percentage to the completion rate to come up with the apprentice rate.

3. Refer to the "IRA Compliance Mastery" course for details on coming up with the prevailing wage.

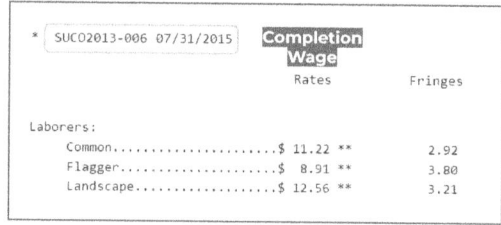

Look up the completion wage, then apply a discount rate to determine the apprentice rate. A good starting point is 70 percent, though this can vary. Check with your state agency for specific guidelines, as they might encourage you to pay closer to the prevailing wage. Generally, 70 percent is a safe bet.

Wage Progression Evaluations

Once you've set your starting wage, defined your wage progressions, and established your completion wage, it's crucial to ensure no milestones slip through the cracks. After all, we're talking about someone's pay, and it's essential that nothing is overlooked.

To manage this effectively, set clear milestones for wage progression eligibility. Determine the triggers—are they based on hours worked, course completions, competency achievements, or a combination? When an apprentice reaches a wage progression milestone, you need a systematic way to assess their eligibility.

For example, let's say an apprentice has completed two thousand hours and is eligible for a wage increase. You should verify that they've completed the required classroom hours and participated actively in their courses. Create an assessment process that documents the criteria and includes a final question: is this apprentice receiving the wage increase? A simple yes or no will suffice.

Pro Tip: Assess Anyone in Apprentix

In Apprentix, you can set up templated assessments and assess anyone on the platform. An assessment allows you to create a custom list of questions and a custom list of answer options. When assessing someone on a wage progression, it's a good idea to make your final question very clear so that audits are easy. Add the question "Are we awarding this apprentice the wage increase?" Many companies automatically award the wage increase when the conditions are met, but some prefer to add this assessment step.

Store all assessment data within Apprentix, and if you choose, share the results with the apprentice or keep them private. This documentation ensures clarity and accountability regarding why an apprentice did or didn't receive a wage increase. Once you've decided to grant the wage increase, make sure to notify payroll so the raise is reflected on the apprentice's paycheck.

That wraps up wage increases. I hope you have a good idea of how you're going to set the starting wages, the completion wages, and the wage increases, regardless of whether you're running a registered or standard apprenticeship. You should be able to construct this in a way that matches what you pay people anyway, both at the starting level and the completion level, and use wage increases as an incentive structure to dangle carrots so that the apprentice continues to move along and progress.

Budgeting Bootcamp

In this chapter, we're going to discuss the essential details of budgeting for an apprenticeship program. Many apprenticeship programs fail due to poor financial planning and an inability to generate a return on investment, so understanding and accurately planning for program costs is critical to ensure the success and sustainability of your program. By the end of this chapter, you'll have a clear understanding of the various expenses involved, the strategies to minimize costs, and how to effectively manage your program using tools like Apprentix. Let's get started.

How Much Does an Apprenticeship Program Cost?

Accurate financial planning is crucial for the success of your apprenticeship programs. Many businesses launch programs that eventually fail, often because they don't generate a return on investment. Understanding the cost structure is key. In this section, we'll discuss the costs involved and how to create the minimum effective dose—the lowest-cost way to achieve the results you want. Additionally, we'll highlight how using Apprentix can streamline your program, help you efficiently manage it, and keep it affordable. Let's dive into the budgeting process.

Program-Level Expenses

Operating an apprenticeship program involves various expenses, categorized as program-level and project-level costs. Program-level expenses are akin to your operating overhead costs. Regardless of whether you're running a registered or unregistered apprenticeship, these costs will be ubiquitous, with some specific to compliance for registered programs.

I put together a budget template that contains all this information that you can download at https://training.apprentix.io/budgeting-bootcamp. I'm going to walk you through all the fields in the template so that you know exactly how to fill it out and what to look for internally so that you can fill this out correctly.

Program Sponsor Costs

The first expense is program sponsor costs. The program sponsor can be an internal person, someone hired externally, or a Fractional Sponsor from Apprentix. This person is responsible for all sponsor duties and ensuring that the program runs smoothly and remains compliant. Allocating these resources appropriately is crucial for your program's success.

Program Admin Costs

The program admin and sponsor can be the same person or two different individuals. Each occupation requires its own program, which means you can have the same sponsor and admin across multiple programs or different people for each. Proper allocation of these resources is necessary for managing costs effectively.

Classroom Costs

Classroom-related costs include the instructor's time, whether they are hired or allocated internally; classroom space rental; and the materials needed to run the class. These costs are essential to ensure that the training environment is conducive to learning.

Insurance Coverage

Insurance coverage typically includes liability and other necessary policies for your employees. If your apprenticeship program requires additional specific insurance, those costs need to be included in your budget.

Software

Using software can significantly improve your program's efficiency. Apprentix is an apprenticeship management system, and you might also investigate adding a learning management system to organize online classes for apprentices. This was discussed in the "Coursework Designer" chapter.

Quality Assurance

The cost of quality assurance includes the cost to regularly perform quality assurance checks and the cost of implementing improvements. This ensures that your program continuously evolves and improves.

Certification and Accreditation Fees

Certification and accreditation fees vary depending on the industry-specific certificates your apprentices need to earn. These costs must be accounted for to ensure your apprentices meet all necessary qualifications.

Affirmative Action Plan and EEO Compliance

Creating and implementing an affirmative action plan and ensuring EEO compliance may involve costs, especially if you bring in external trainers. Budgeting for these expenses ensures that your program meets all regulatory requirements.

Project-Level Expenses

Project-level expenses are operational and tactical and relate to the day-to-day running of the apprenticeship program.

Wages for Apprentices and Wage Increases

The primary cost here is the wages for apprentices, including any planned wage increases. These must be budgeted accurately to ensure the financial viability of your program.

Training and Educational Materials

The cost of training and educational materials refers to the cost of materials that will be used in the classroom and includes any type of capital equipment purchases, time to deliver training, and books. This is distinct from classroom costs, as it pertains to individual needs.

Wages for Instructors and Mentors

Allocate funds for instructors and mentors. Mentors take time away from their productive work to teach, so their time must be valued and budgeted accordingly.

Recruitment

Recruitment costs for apprentices are the same as for hiring any new employee. Include these costs in your budget to ensure you can attract the best candidates.

Travel and Transportation

If apprentices need to travel for training or on-the-job experience, those costs must be included. Budgeting for travel and transportation ensures that apprentices can access necessary training locations.

A Word of Caution about Building Grants into Your Budget

Some of these expenses can be offset through grants and funding in a registered program. When pursuing grants and funding, you have a couple of options. You can build the expectation of grant funding into your budget—though I would caution you to do this very conservatively because, as you probably know, grants are not guaranteed and might not come in at the amounts you apply for. They are a variable, whereas a budget is a fixed number. If you are applying for enough grants, you might be able to anticipate a certain amount that you would be comfortable budgeting for. Nonprofits do this all the time, and businesses can do it too, but most businesses aren't prolific in pursuing grants.

Instead, do not budget for grant funding but rather use it to offset costs when you receive it. Relying too heavily on grant funding can be problematic if it dries up, which is a major reason some businesses' apprenticeship programs fail. If grant funding disappears and the program is no longer sustainable without it, the program may be cut. Therefore, it's best to make your apprenticeship program worthwhile for the business without depending on grant funding. When you do receive grants, they become an added bonus, or "gravy." Determine what's appropriate for your business and plan accordingly.

How to Include Apprenticeship Costs in Your Bids

How do you work the overhead cost of the apprenticeship program and the variable cost of the actual apprentices into a bid? Use the overhead cost as part of a markup.

Effectively, when you have operational overhead, you can add a percentage to your labor hours. By marking that up, you incorporate the overhead costs into your bid. Take the apprenticeship program overhead cost and create a percentage that is specifically the markup for your workers. That way, when you add the apprentices' wages into the bid, you also include a markup that covers a portion of the operational overhead related to those apprentices.

You'll have to be specific when crunching the numbers, but don't forget that it's not just the apprentices on the ground in a project you're bidding on. There's also the overhead, and that overhead should be included in the bid.

That wraps up the budgeting process. Here's the download link again for the budgeting template so you can start filling it out: https://training.apprentix.io/budgeting-bootcamp.

My goal here is to help you create the minimum effective dose for your apprenticeship program. By "dose," I mean the lowest-cost way to achieve the results your business needs—like the minimum viable product (MVP) concept we discussed earlier. This doesn't mean cutting all costs to the bone and operating at no cost other than wages. That's not realistic. You will incur some costs because investing in the program is necessary to generate a return on investment.

Technology in the Apprentix platform is one of the ways you can make a highly leveraged investment—there's a great deal of return on that technology for your program. That's one area to consider. Another area where Apprentix can help is with the Fractional Sponsor. Instead of allocating someone internally who might be better off doing other work or hiring someone externally to handle compliance, you can bring in someone from our team as a Fractional Sponsor. This person would be responsible for your program and compliance, but you don't have to pay them as a full-time employee. It's a tiny fraction of the cost because you need them for only specific responsibilities, and we can do it at scale.

In this chapter, we've covered the various expenses involved in running an apprenticeship program and how to effectively budget for them. By understanding these costs and planning accordingly, you can ensure the success and sustainability of your program. Tools like Apprentix can help streamline the process and reduce costs, making your apprenticeship program more efficient and effective. Remember, accurate budgeting and resource allocation are key to generating a return on investment and achieving the desired outcomes for your business.

Recruiting Apprentices

Finding the right apprentices is crucial for the success of your apprenticeship program. In this chapter, we'll explore various methods to recruit apprentices, the importance of skills-based recruiting, and the key roles required to effectively support your apprenticeship program. By the end, you'll have a comprehensive strategy to attract and manage top talent in your apprenticeship program.

Current Crew

Look for someone who's been with your company for six months or less. This pool of candidates is ideal for apprentices because they're still new. They certainly would benefit from a lot of training, and they're still moldable. They're new to your company, so they will appreciate being enrolled in an apprenticeship program. Somebody who's been a part of the business for a long time might think, "Why would I go through an apprenticeship unless it's to progress and upskill into another role?" They're more likely to be resistant if you try to apprentice them in their current role, so target those who are more junior in your company—not necessarily in age but in tenure.

Direct Entry

Direct entry methods for bringing in apprentices are straightforward ways to get candidates into your apprenticeship program without a lot of prescreening or extra training programs. Your program must be open to candidates regardless of race, ethnicity, religion, national origin, or sex.

1. Job Corps Graduates

Youths who have completed a Job Corps training program in any occupation covered in your apprenticeship standards and who meet the minimum qualifications can be directly admitted into your program. If no apprentice openings are available, they can be placed at the top of the current applicant list and given the first opportunity for placement. Evaluate their Job Corps training to grant appropriate credit on the term of the apprenticeship.

2. YouthBuild Graduates

Like Job Corps graduates, YouthBuild graduates who meet the minimum qualifications can be directly admitted or placed at the top of the applicant list. Evaluate their training to grant credit for previous experience.

3. Military Veterans

Veterans registered with Helmets to Hardhats and those who have completed military technical training or participated in a registered apprenticeship program while in the military can be given direct entry. Evaluate their military training to grant appropriate credit and determine their wage rate. Veterans must provide a DD-214 to verify their training and experience.

4. Former Inmates

Individuals who have participated in or completed a specific Bureau of Prisons apprenticeship program can be directly admitted into your apprenticeship program. This should be done without regard to current qualifications, eligibility lists, or test scores.

5. Employees of Nonsignatory Employers

Employees of a nonsignatory employer who do not qualify as journey workers when the employer becomes signatory can be evaluated and registered at the appropriate period of apprenticeship based on previous work experience and related training. If they don't qualify for credit, they must apply through normal procedures.

6. Organizing Efforts

Employees who sign authorization cards during an organizing effort and do not qualify as journey workers can be evaluated and registered based on previous experience. They must meet specific requirements such as being employed in the sponsor's jurisdiction and providing reliable documentation of their employment.

7. Senior Community Service Employment Program (SCSEP) Graduates

Seniors who have completed an SCSEP pre-apprenticeship training program in any health care occupation covered in your standards and who meet the minimum qualifications can be admitted directly into your program. If no apprentice openings are available, they can be placed at the top of the applicant list. Evaluate their SCSEP training to grant appropriate credit on the term of apprenticeship.

8. Pre-Apprenticeship Program Graduates

Individuals who have completed a structured pre-apprenticeship program that meets specific quality standards can be directly admitted into your apprenticeship program. They must provide documentation confirming the completion of the pre-apprenticeship program. Evaluate their training to grant appropriate credit. The great thing about pre-apprentices is that they've already demonstrated an interest and commitment to the occupation and they've completed a portion of the classroom training that you won't have to teach or pay for.

Skills-Based Recruiting

Skills-based recruiting involves using skills-based job descriptions and skills ratings in your hiring process. It's a game changer. Instead of focusing solely on résumés and job titles, you look at the specific skills and competencies a candidate brings to the table. This method can uncover hidden talents and ensure you're hiring the right person for the right job.

Imagine you're hiring for a tech role. Instead of just looking for someone with a software developer title, you use a skills-based approach to find candidates who excel in specific programming languages, problem solving, and project management. This approach can broaden your talent pool and bring in candidates who might not have the traditional background but have the exact skills you need.

Using Apprentix's skills-based job description builder, you can automate this process based on job titles. It's a powerful tool that helps you create detailed job descriptions focusing on the skills required, ensuring you attract the best candidates. Skills-based recruiting also allows for better matching of apprentices to the roles they're best suited for, enhancing their training and development.

Key Roles

Now let's go through the key roles you need to fill for your apprenticeship program. We've already talked about needing a program sponsor for each program. You're also going to need a program admin for each program. Yes, the sponsor and admin can be the same person and they can handle multiple programs, but these are distinct roles that need to be named.

- **Managers** are responsible for approving timecards and marking competencies as complete after evaluating the apprentice. These are often journey workers, supervisors, or team leads. They play a crucial role in day-to-day oversight.
- **Mentors** provide feedback, advice, and guidance. While a mentor can also be a journey worker, their primary job is to support and coach the apprentice, not necessarily to approve their progress.
- **Instructors** are responsible for teaching the classroom materials—the theory, not the on-the-job training. This could be someone online, a local professor, or an instructor at a training center.
- **Apprentices** are the core of your program, the ones who will benefit from and contribute to the training and development you provide.

In Apprentix, these roles are clearly defined and essential for recordkeeping. Each role must stamp their approval on the data to ensure a clear audit trail, showing who has done what and approved what.

Recruiting apprentices is about finding the right people and setting them up for success. Whether you're looking within your current crew, exploring direct entry methods, or using skills-based recruiting, having a clear strategy is key. With the right roles filled and processes in place, your apprenticeship program will thrive.

Next, we'll dive into how to schedule apprentices effectively, ensuring they get the most out of their training while contributing to your business.

Scheduling Apprentices

In this chapter, I'm going to walk you through how to schedule your apprentices because that can be a challenge depending on your work schedule. I want to make sure that you incorporate the apprentices into your actual work schedule and that you carve out the least time so that the full apprenticeship is integrated with your actual work, making it the most efficient.

How Do I Find Time for All of This?

When setting up your apprenticeship, one of the most common questions you're going to face is when to schedule the classroom time and the on-the-job training time for the apprentice. Start by looking at the apprentice's current shifts. What is their baseline working hours? Next, check if you already have regular training sessions scheduled. If you do, integrate your apprenticeship training with these existing sessions.

Once that's sorted, move on to scheduling the coursework. Apprentices can do coursework during the day or after work. Downtime, such as during bad weather when outdoor work might stop, is a perfect time for apprentices to hop on their phones and complete some courses.

Can Apprentices Do Coursework on Their Own Time?

Yes, apprentices can complete coursework in their spare time, both during and after work hours. But do you have to pay apprentices for their class time? The answer is no. Most businesses have apprentices do coursework on their own time to put some skin in the game, especially since the business is already covering the cost of the coursework and on-the-job training.

Do You Have to Pay for On-the-Job Training and Transportation Time?

Yes, you do. An apprenticeship is a job, so when they're working and training on the job, you pay for that time. But what about transit time? If apprentices are traveling to a course at a training center or community college, you pay them for mileage, but not for the time spent in transit. Also, transit time doesn't count toward classroom hours. If they spend two hours driving and three hours in class, only the three hours count.

How Many Hours a Week Does Coursework Take?

Many organizations have new-hire orientations, and all this classroom time counts toward the minimum classroom hours required. This time is often front loaded before the apprentice begins on-the-job training. Typically, apprentices spend about two to three hours a week in class.

In a registered apprenticeship program, you need 144 minimum classroom hours per 2,000 hours on the job—2,000 hours are basically 40 hours a week for 50 weeks, roughly one year. So, in a year, apprentices need to spend at least 144 hours in the classroom. That breaks down to about three hours per week, though this can be flexible. Some weeks might be five hours, others two, depending on the schedule.

Can the Schedule Be Flexible?

Absolutely. But the more predictable the schedule is for the apprentice, the more likely they are to complete the coursework. It helps to keep a consistent schedule instead of constantly shifting their hours.

What Is the Ratio of On-the-Job to Classroom Hours?

If you have a 3,000-hour apprenticeship, you still need only 144 classroom hours. But for a 4,000-hour apprenticeship, you need 288 classroom hours. For competency-based apprenticeships, it's usually a minimum of 144 classroom hours for the first 2,000 hours. The duration will depend on how quickly the apprentice completes their competencies, but it must be at least 2,000 hours. For hybrid apprenticeships, you calculate the classroom hours to fit the maximum number of hours in the apprenticeship. For a 3,000- to 4,000-hour apprenticeship, you need 288 classroom hours, even if the apprentice completes it in 3,000 hours. If your program isn't registered, you have more flexibility to decide the ratios that work best for you.

Pro Tip: Customize Apprentix for All Training Types

In Apprentix, select the occupation and training type, and a message will display the required hours or range of hours for the registered apprenticeship. This way, you know upfront if this is the right occupation for your business.

How Is Progress Monitored and Documented?

Monitor the apprentice's progress and time every week. Track how many hours they've completed in coursework and on-the-job training and which competencies they've been evaluated on. This can be done using a system like Apprentix, or even with spreadsheets or paper, though the latter might be less organized. Ensure you're not just relying on payroll hours; you need to specifically allocate time to on-the-job training and classroom hours.

Can Apprentices Work on Different Projects at the Same Time?

Yes, apprentices can work on multiple projects, but ensure each project offers on-the-job training. If an apprentice splits their time between two projects, make sure both projects contribute to their training. Otherwise, they might fall behind in their on-the-job training hours.

When scheduling apprentices, aim for a consistent schedule as much as possible. Set clear expectations for how many hours per week they'll spend in class and on the job, and have a system to track all this. Integrate their training into their regular work to leverage your existing workflow without disrupting operations. This approach reduces operational overhead and ensures the apprenticeship program is seamlessly built into your business.

***

Now that you've designed your apprenticeship program, you're ready to launch! And if you are required to or interested in having a *registered* apprenticeship program, continue to the next section. If not, skip it and just check out the "Calls to Action" section at the end of the book.

Section IV: Registered Apprenticeships

There are roughly one million apprentices in the United States. Only half are enrolled in programs registered with the government. The rest are enrolled in programs that operate independently.

But bureaucrats want you to believe in only *registered* apprenticeships. They say, "If it's not registered, it's not really an apprenticeship." They were given this line by unions who lobbied for the Fitzgerald Act in 1937. They say registration is the only way to ensure a high-quality apprenticeship. This is completely and utterly false today.

When you create an apprenticeship using the steps in this book, you've created a high-quality apprenticeship. You could click a button in Apprentix to register your apprenticeship, yet over half of businesses choose not to. Why is that? Because the government's value prop for registration hasn't been strong enough. The incentives haven't been worth the strings attached.

That's why bureaucrats came up with a new strategy: mandating apprenticeships. Certain federal, state, and local laws require you to have an apprenticeship. So if you're *required* to have a registered apprenticeship program, this section is for you. Or if you're *interested* in having a registered apprenticeship program, this section is for you. However, if you simply want to create a high-quality apprenticeship program without the bureaucracy, you don't need to register your program. Skip this section and move on to "Calls to Action."

Let's dive in.

The System

What is a <u>registered</u> apprenticeship?

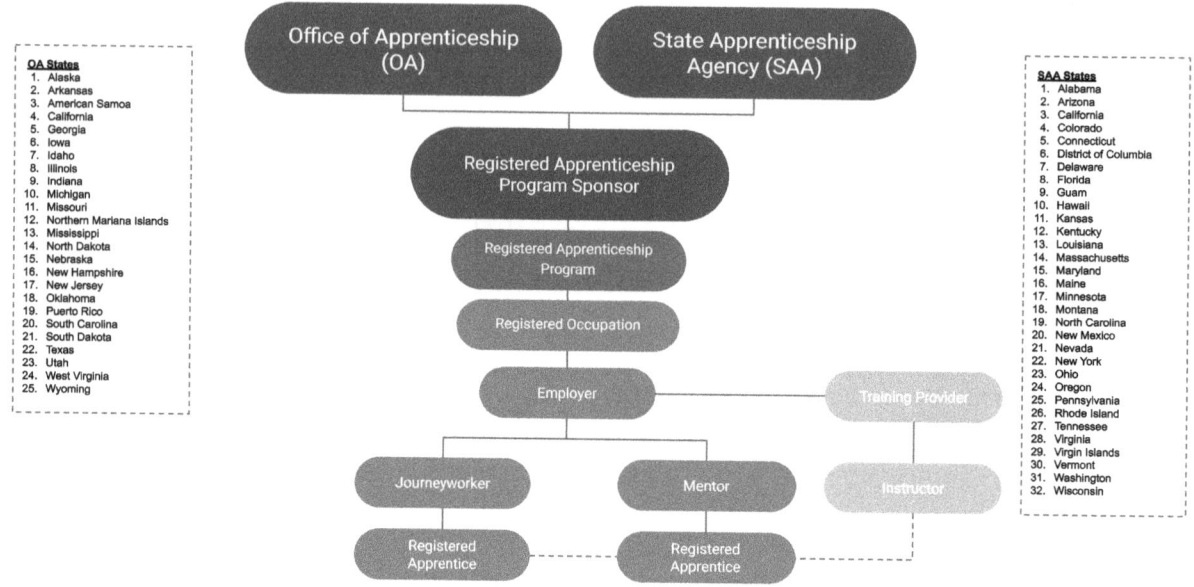

Two types of government offices are in charge of registered apprenticeship programs. This is called the National Apprenticeship System, a.k.a. the system.

Governing Bodies: OA vs. SAA

Office of Apprenticeships (OA) states account for roughly half of US states and territories. OA states all have the same standardized set of rules and standards, and they all work together and use the same databases. Each state does have rules and standards that might be slightly tweaked here and there, but they are federally funded and all operate together. In contrast, State Apprenticeship Agencies (SAA) states operate autonomously—sort of. What that means is that the DoL has said, "Okay, state, you can operate with your own set of rules. You can use your own standards. You can use your own database if you want. You can use ours too if you want, but you can do your own thing." Why do certain states do this? There's a whole list of reasons that we don't necessarily need to go into, but basically, it's so that they can operate however they want.

The image above shows a list of all the OA and SAA states and territories. This list is current as of the writing of this book, but you can find an updated list on the ApprenticeshipUSA website at https://www.apprenticeship.gov/about-us/apprenticeship-system. As you can see, roughly half are OA states and half are SAA states. This is critical for you to understand, because the process for registration varies based on whether you register in an OA or SAA state.

For example, let's say we're headquartered in Georgia, an OA state. We want to register our apprenticeship within Georgia and then expand our program when we start a new project in Oregon. Oregon is an SAA state. There isn't necessarily a reciprocal agreement that says, "I'm already registered in Georgia; therefore, I should qualify to be registered in Oregon." It doesn't work that way. You'd have to register in

Oregon. The registration process, which we'll dive into, means that you'll have to do something different for one state versus the other state.

Common Terminology

So now that we understand the governing bodies, if you will, let's look at the terms you're going to encounter.

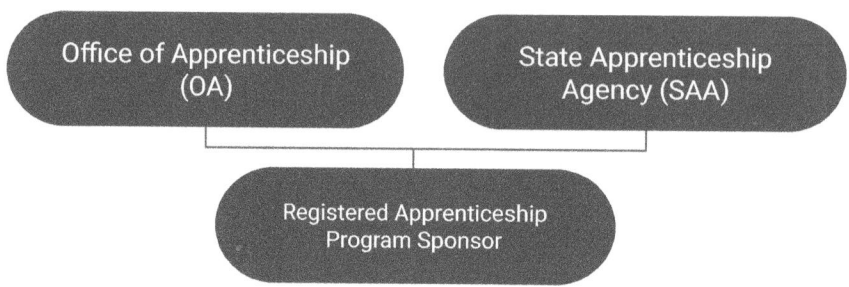

Registered Apprenticeship Program Sponsor

The registered apprenticeship program sponsor is responsible for all sorts of activities to ensure that the program is running smoothly and is in compliance with either the OA or the SAA, or both if you have multiple programs in multiple states. The sponsor has a whole set of duties, which we outline in the next chapter, "Program Sponsor Playbook." The sponsor is at the top level when it comes to registered apprenticeship programs.

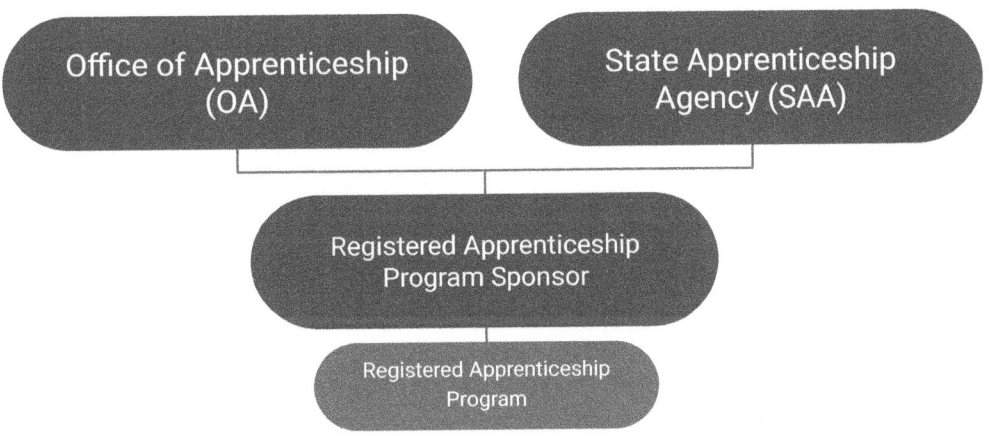

Registered Apprenticeship Program

The registered apprenticeship program is an arrangement that says you agree to abide by the guidelines set by the system for any occupations you decide to register. A program typically is registered in each state in which you operate and defines which occupations have been registered. Multiple occupations can be registered under a single program.

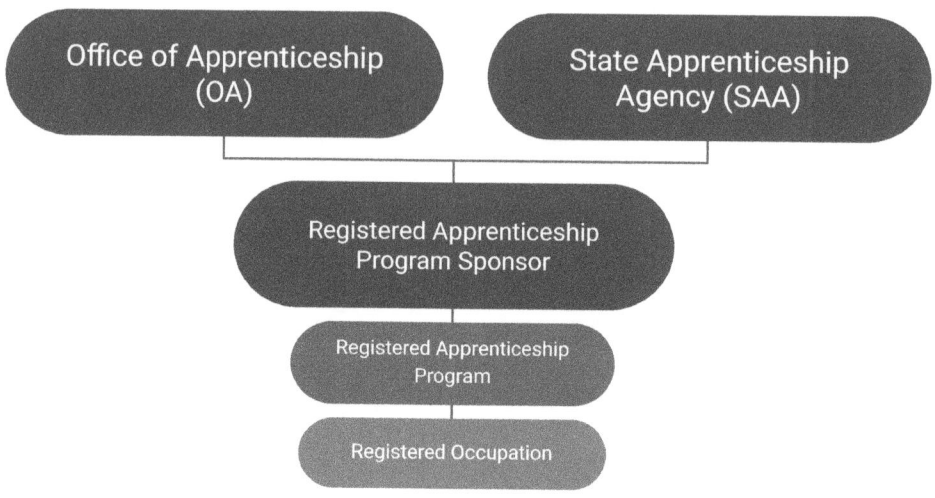

Registered Occupation

Let's say you wanted to create apprenticeships in heavy equipment and craft labor. Each occupation will be listed under your program. Each program will be under a sponsor. And generally speaking, each state will require you to register your own program.

Now, you might think, "Well, can't I just have one program that works for me in multiple states?" You can if the occupation or occupations you want to register don't require separate licensure by each state. For example, if you have a registered apprenticeship program for an electrician, it is not eligible to be a national program because each state has different licensure requirements, which in turn means that you'd have to register a different program for each state. Typically, occupations in the trades aren't eligible for a national program.

You could apply for National Guideline Standards (NGS) certification at the federal level. You'd then take this certification to each state, and they should in theory fast-track your registration because the federal government already reviewed your apprenticeship standards and paperwork and said it looks good. With your NGS certification, an OA state is typically able to register you quickly because they are federal employees, whereas SAA states may or may not consider your NGS certification when registering your program.

Additionally, some programs can be registered as meeting National Program Standards (NPS) to be recognized in all states. However, this is available only to occupations that don't require state-by-state licensure. If that's you and you intend to scale across multiple states, you may want to pursue this approach from the very beginning.

Now, here's the thing: Each program applies to as many projects or as many work streams as you want in whichever states you're registered. Let's say you have a registered apprenticeship program with the craft laborers occupation. You can have multiple crews of craft laborers working on multiple projects all under one program, provided those crews are working in the same state. Those crews cannot travel to another state without you having a registered apprenticeship program in that state as well, unless you have an NPS program. Therefore, if you have projects in different states, you will need to repeat the registration process in each state. Yup, one program per state, and each occupation must be registered where you want apprentices.

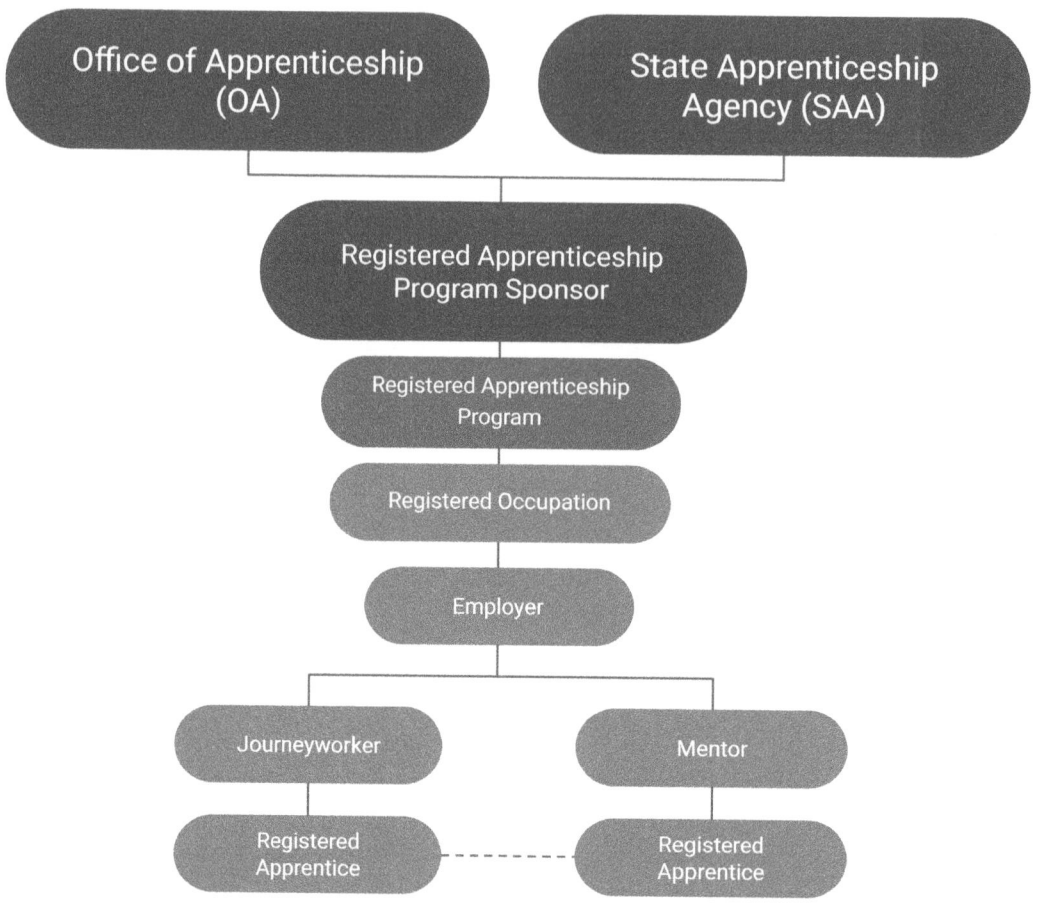

Employers (a.k.a. Businesses)

Underpinning a program is what they call employers. I have a bone to pick with the use of the term *employer* because, frankly, businesses are businesses—they're not in the business of employment. They employ people to be in business.

The governing bodies want to call businesses employers, so that's what they do. So below the registered occupation is the employer. One registered occupation can have multiple employers under it or just one employer under it. This is why it is important to see how this thing breaks down.

Program Admin

Each program must have a sponsor and an admin. We've already discussed the sponsor a few paragraphs above at the start of this section. However, there's also the point of contact at the employer who is responsible for the day-to-day operations of the program, and that person is known as the program admin.

Yes, the sponsor and admin can both be the same person, and yes, the sponsor and admin can be the same person across multiple programs. But you do need to have named a sponsor and an admin for each program because each one of the programs will have its own compliance and operational needs.

This is where the complexity starts to increase exponentially. If you have three programs, you're going to have three times the amount of compliance work. If you have one program, you're just going to have compliance work for only one. Thus, it is in your best interest to have a program cover the greatest number of apprentices possible.

For example, let's say you're planning to register three occupations under your registered apprenticeship program: construction laborers, heavy equipment operators, and electricians. Now let's say that you need only one construction laborer apprentice, but you need five heavy equipment operator apprentices and five electrician apprentices. You might consider not having an apprenticeship program for that one construction laborer because the cost of operating that will likely not have a great ROI relative to the cost of operating the programs with five apprentices in each.

In this example, you'd be better off registering two occupations: the operator and electrician. Now, if you must have that third occupation by law because you're going to have to fulfill certain project requirements and there is one person who must be an apprentice, then you must have it. There's no way around it. What you can do, of course, is share the costs of the sponsor and admin across all three programs, but it will become a shared-services cost across all of them.

Journeymen

Part of an apprenticeship is that the apprentice is learning under someone more experienced. This person is known as a journeyman. You might have different internal titles for them in your business, such as team leads, supervisors, managers, or mentors, but they are people who have been there, have done that, and can teach the apprentice.

Registered Apprentice

An apprentice in a registered apprenticeship program is called a registered apprentice, because they sign an agreement with the business saying that they're in this apprenticeship program. While similar, a registered apprentice differs from a registered apprenticeship.

Mentors

The mentor in an apprenticeship program is a trusted guide, a source of wisdom, an emotional supporter, a skills developer, a connector, and an advocate. They provide a holistic approach to the apprentice's personal and professional growth. Through their mentorship, they ensure that the apprentice not only masters the trade but also evolves into a confident, capable, and connected professional.

Mentors may or may not be journeymen, but a mentor should not be the apprentice's supervisor. Ideally, the mentor role is separate from that of the supervisor.

A good mentor embodies a blend of extensive experience, effective communication, and a genuine commitment to their mentee's growth. Effective communication is key, with a good mentor conveying ideas and feedback clearly while actively listening to the mentee's concerns. Mentors provide balanced constructive feedback, focusing on strengths and areas for improvement while offering solutions and support. Through these qualities, a good mentor effectively guides their mentee, fostering personal and professional growth.

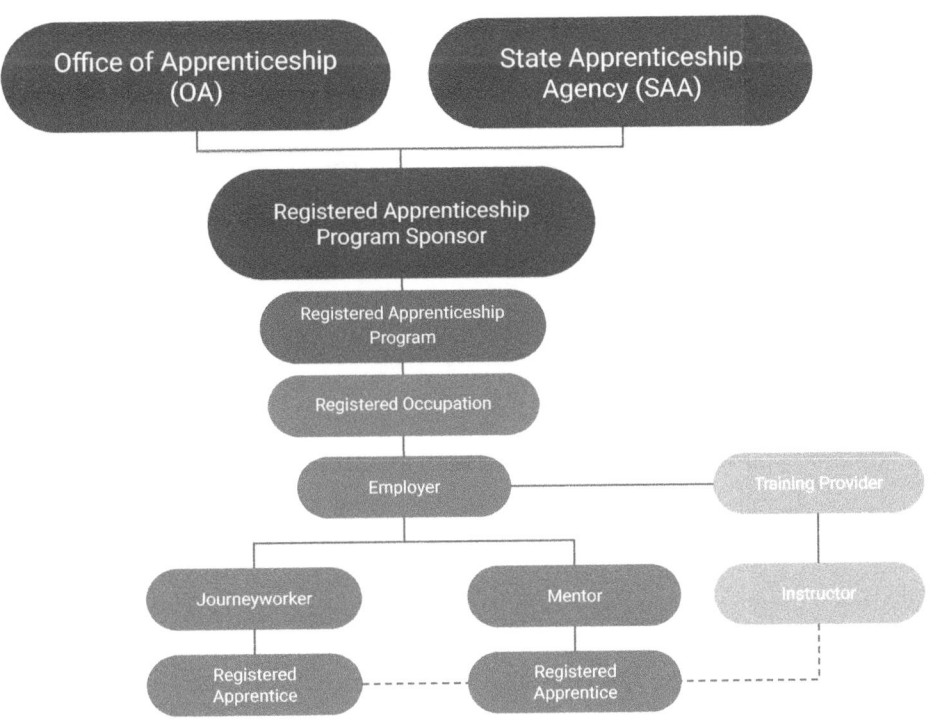

Training Provider

The training provider is the organization that will be responsible for delivering the curriculum. The training provider can be your company or a third party such as an online school, local training center, community college, or four-year university. There's a whole list of ways that people can buy training, but the training provider is a separate role.

Instructors

Under the training provider are instructors who teach the registered apprentices. Instructors are responsible for delivering the curriculum and are the names listed on the apprentices' official transcripts, along with the training provider. The instructor takes attendance, delivers the curriculum, and assesses the apprentices to ensure the knowledge is being retained.

So when people say, "Do you have a registered apprenticeship?" it's an incomplete question. The technical answer is "Our business has a registered apprenticeship program for these occupations under this sponsor, where apprentices are taught in the classroom by someone and on the job by someone more senior." But let's keep it real, you're not really going to say that, so just say, "Yeah, we do."

Can One Person Serve in Multiple Roles?

In a registered apprenticeship program, it is indeed possible for one person to fulfill multiple roles such as sponsor, administrator, mentor, trainer, and instructor. However, while overlapping roles can simplify operations and reduce administrative overhead, it is essential to consider the implications for program effectiveness and compliance.

For instance, a sponsor, typically responsible for the overall management and compliance of the apprenticeship program, might also take on the role of an administrator who handles day-to-day operations and communication with regulatory bodies. Meanwhile, the mentor focuses on guiding and supporting the apprentice's personal and professional development, providing a distinct yet complementary layer of support. A trainer or journeyman offers hands-on technical training, ensuring that the apprentice acquires the necessary skills through practical application. Finally, an instructor delivers the educational curriculum, assessing apprentices to ensure knowledge retention.

Combining roles can be practical in smaller programs or organizations with limited staff, but each role has unique demands and responsibilities that contribute to a comprehensive apprenticeship experience. While one person can juggle roles, it might not be the best approach if you want clear responsibilities and efficient management. Separating the roles can provide clarity and focus, enhancing the apprentice's learning journey.

Navigating the intricacies of the system means understanding the distinct roles and responsibilities required for a successful program. We've talked about the OA states working under a unified set of standards and the SAA states having the autonomy to do their own thing. This distinction matters because it influences how you register and manage your programs, whether you're in one state or many.

Low-Value Claims on Why You Should Register

Government-funded bureaucrats claim the reason to register your apprenticeship program is to receive benefits available only to those who register. Unfortunately, the value proposition for these benefits is often no better than just claims. With each claim, it's important to know what you'll truly receive to see if it's worth it for your business. I'll share with you the complaints I hear from Apprentix customers so that if you decide to pursue registration, you'll be able to ask an educated set of questions, having been made aware that the claim itself needs substantiation.

Claim 1: Recruiting Assistance to Fill Your Jobs

One of the reasons bureaucrats will tell you to register your apprenticeship program is because they say that you can get assistance to recruit your apprentices. Let me tell you where they're recruiting from: the unemployment office. Are there workers there in a 3 percent unemployment economy? Some. Are they the ones who want to work? Probably not. So are you pulling from the best pool of high-potential candidates? Probably not.

Is that a realistic value proposition for you? You'd have to assess it. You might have a great workforce center that does a whole lot more outreach than just being the rebranded unemployment office. But for the most part, nationwide, they're pulling from a pool of candidates who are unemployed.

Apprentix customers have been quick to point out that workforce centers are often so resource strapped that they don't deliver timely candidates who meet their requirements, so you'll want to get a better sense of who will be helping, how much capacity they have to recruit for you, what their service-level agreements are, and what their expected timelines are.

Claim 2: Help Creating Your Apprenticeship Program

Bureaucrats will say, "We'll help you create your apprenticeship program." Oh Lord, let me tell you how long that takes: nine to twelve months! I'm speaking from experience. You'll endure rounds and rounds of back-and-forth communications, forty-eight email threads between you and the apprenticeship training representative, with no systems in place to make the process more efficient. You'll constantly hear the refrain "We're understaffed," because of a supposed workload queue that's so long.

The resource issue is exacerbated by the fact that the government has poured hundreds of millions into funding apprenticeship intermediaries, leading the people who work in government apprenticeship offices to leave for higher-paid roles with these intermediaries. Imagine that—the government just paid to hire away its own team!

The irony is that apprenticeships are all about training people in theory and hands-on application, but the very people who administer apprenticeships for the state have received very little training themselves. To further complicate matters, these folks aren't in the business of starting or running a business, or even an apprenticeship program. Yet they are supposed to provide you with assistance. They barely know what it takes to run an apprenticeship program. They're probably reading this book too.

When they say they can help you start an apprenticeship program, they're just following a playbook step by step. If you don't know how to answer everything in their playbook, their ability to help is limited. Sure, some states have apprenticeship liaisons who are a bit more customer friendly. If you find one, go for it.

But let me warn you, it is mind-numbing and overwhelming. They bombard you with information without strategically curating it to your specific needs, and their response times are frustratingly slow. You'll likely burn out before you ever get anything started. So the help they offer is essentially the government's version of help—bureaucratic, slow, and often inefficient.

Claim 3: National Credential for Apprentices

Bureaucrats say that the national credential apprentices earn is valuable in the marketplace. Unfortunately, outside of the trades and health care, very few industries and companies really care. If a candidate walks in with a DoL certificate, it doesn't mean much. We have over one million credentials in the United States alone. So, when someone walks in and says, "I've earned this certificate in blah, blah, blah," I don't know if it's legit, and you don't know if it's legit.

In the trades and health care, they might know whether it's legit or not, but it doesn't automatically add value. What you really want is someone who walks in your door, and if they've been through an apprenticeship program, you want to know if they can do the job. They might say, "I've gone through this apprenticeship program," and that's great; you might trust that they know how to do the job. But just because they've earned a certificate doesn't mean it carries weight with businesses when there are over a million different credentials in the United States.

Don't assume the DoL's credential means something to your apprentices if what they really care about is making more money and working at a company that invests in their future.

Claim 4: National Recognition

The DoL . . . sorry, but it doesn't exactly have the brand it's claiming. No one's in awe thinking, "Oh, wow, that's impressive." It's the DoL. It says, "There's national recognition for your company if you have a registered apprenticeship program," because it will post your company's name in an online database.

Who cares? Literally no one cares. Having your company's name posted online will do nothing for your business. If the DoL understood marketing at all, it would know that posting your name on a website with thousands of other companies, with no distinguishing characteristics between one company and another and no website traffic, does nothing for you. It will not generate leads. It will not create brand awareness. There is literally no benefit.

Although the DoL claims it will give you recognition, no one cares. It's not even recognition that moves outside of the DoL's little sphere. If it brought brand awareness to your market, that would be fantastic, but I'm sorry, that's not what happens.

Claim 5: High-Quality Standards

Apprenticeship governing bodies claim to uphold high-quality standards, but when you look at what they write versus what it takes to operate a program, the reality is vastly different. They don't uphold high-quality standards; they just require you to fill out forms that make it look like you do. At no point in the registered apprenticeship process do they monitor whether you've done the necessary tasks until they conduct an audit. During the audit, they check your compliance. It's not about maintaining high-quality standards—it's about creating the appearance of them through paperwork. They don't help you along the way or check your progress until they audit you and say, "You've messed up." Are these truly advanced quality standards? I don't think so.

You don't need to register your apprenticeship program to have high-quality standards. If you create an apprenticeship within Apprentix, our six-step process will help you generate a program with built-in high-quality standards, whether or not you register it. To say that only registered apprenticeship programs have high-quality standards is a farce.

Claim 6: Ongoing Free, Customized Support

When you create your apprenticeship program, you're essentially set loose to figure everything out on your own. The reason is that all OA and SAA states are incentivized based on certain metrics:

- Number of apprenticeship programs registered
- Number of employers registered
- Number of apprentices who have started programs
- Number of apprentices who have completed programs

The completion part might imply that you get ongoing support to ensure apprentices finish the program. However, the incentives are focused on starts, not completions. The DoL measures completions through its centralized Registered Apprenticeship Partners Information Database System (RAPIDS), but the local organizations that help register the programs and employers are measured only on the setup side of things.

So when you look at that, they say, "We've got you set up. If you need resources, go check out this website," and you can find plenty of information there. The issue isn't the availability of information; the issue is the vast amount of work between starting a program, running it, and ensuring apprentices complete it. And how do you do that? They themselves don't really know because they've not actually run these programs themselves.

To say that there's ongoing support is, unfortunately, another farce. You're left to navigate the complexities on your own without the practical, hands-on guidance you truly need.

How Long Does It Take to Register a Program?

How long does it take to register a program?

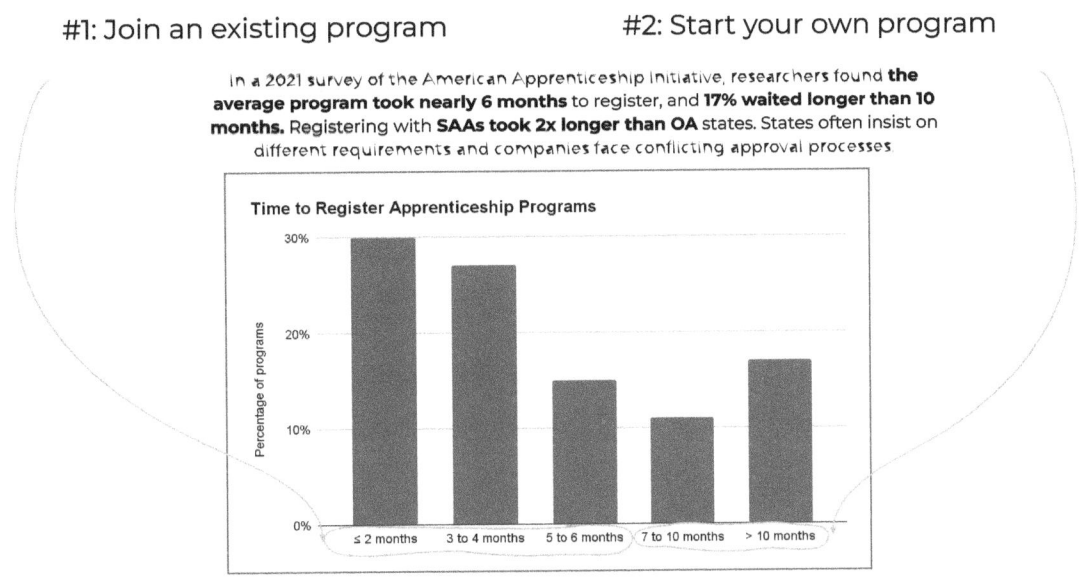

#1: Join an existing program   #2: Start your own program

In a 2021 survey of the American Apprenticeship Initiative, researchers found **the average program took nearly 6 months** to register, and **17% waited longer than 10 months.** Registering with **SAAs took 2x longer than OA** states. States often insist on different requirements and companies face conflicting approval processes.

Time to Register Apprenticeship Programs

It's important for you to understand the timelines you're going to face so that you can plan accordingly. Let's start with what it looks like to join an existing program. Refer back to the diagram at the start of this section just above the section "The System"—there was a registered apprenticeship program sponsor at the top. The timelines differ if you want to join someone's program with them being the sponsor and if you want to start your own program as a sponsor. And then, the timelines also differ if you work within an OA state and if you work within an SAA state. The truth is every single state has different timelines, but research shows that the waiting period is twice as long if you're going through an SAA state than if you're going through an OA state.

In a 2021 survey on the American Apprenticeship Initiative, researchers also found that the average program took nearly six months to register, and 17 percent of people waited over ten months.[13] So, on average, if you're going to join an existing program, you can avoid a lot of work, but it's going to take you, on average, somewhere around three to six months and sometimes over ten months. If you're starting your own program, you're definitely looking at over ten months. And if you are in an SAA state, I'm sorry to tell you, it's likely that it's going to take you twice as long. You would think that an SAA state that operates autonomously could have broken the shackles and made itself more efficient, but lo and behold, that does not appear to be the case.

Three Ways to Get a Registered Apprenticeship Program

There are 3 ways to get a registered apprenticeship

#1: Join an existing program

Pros:

- ☑ Less cost
- ☑ Immediate setup
- ☑ Keep you compliant
- ☑ Not alone

Cons:

- ✕ Less control
- ✕ No tech platform
- ✕ Bureaucratic puppets
- ✕ Unionized labor (if union)
- ✕ High education costs (if college)

#2: Start your own program

Pros:

- ☑ More control
- ☑ Customized
- ☑ No pressure to conform
- ☑ Get your own tech platform

Cons:

- ✕ Higher costs
- ✕ Longer setup
- ✕ Compliance risk
- ✕ Resource intense

You have three options for getting a registered apprenticeship program.

---

[13] Karen Gardiner et al., *Expanding Registered Apprenticeship in the United States: Description of American Apprenticeship Initiative Grantees and Their Programs*, report prepared for the US Department of Labor, Employment and Training Administration (Rockville, MD: Abt Associates and Washington, DC: Urban Institute, September 2021), https://www.dol.gov/sites/dolgov/files/OASP/evaluation/pdf/AAI%20Grant%20Program%20Description_Final.pdf.

Option 1: Join an Existing Program

There are several pros and cons to joining an existing program. If you join an existing program, costs will be lower, setting up will be immediate once you enter the program, the program provider will be able to help keep you compliant, and you won't be alone in all this. The downside is that you'll have less control because you'll have to adhere to their system of operations. They'll have no technology to help you with this. They are effectively bureaucratic puppets. They have been funded to be sponsors, so they receive government funding to be sponsors to multiple employers; therefore, they're going to follow the rules that they're told to follow. And therefore, you must follow the rules they're told to follow. So take it for what it's worth.

Another example of existing programs you can join is unions. Unions fall into the category of an existing program, so if you're looking to join a union, the union will have an existing apprenticeship program and you'll be joining that.

Another group of sponsors consists of education providers, training centers, colleges, community colleges, universities, and so on. When you're looking to get education for your apprentices, education costs will be higher. These sponsors also receive government funding to be sponsors, and their job is to convince companies to join their programs because they can provide the education, which they obviously charge people for. If they convince companies to join their programs, they're making their money. Consequently, the cost of education might not be the lowest because you're joining someone's existing program and they'll deliver the education if they're the sponsor.

Option 2: Start Your Own Program

The pros to starting your own program are effectively the opposite of the cons of joining an existing program: You'll have more control. You'll be able to customize the program to what you want it to be. There's no pressure to conform because you're not taking anybody's money. And you can purchase your own tech platform like Apprentix.

You could say, "We want to use Apprentix to do this." If you're joining someone else's program, you might be able to use Apprentix, but that program sponsor might not want you to. They'll probably say, "Look, we do things the way we do things. Here's your spreadsheet, here's your clipboard, and here's your paper and pen." So if you're starting your own program, you'll have the ability to purchase Apprentix to help you streamline all these processes.

The downsides are that costs are higher, it takes longer, and compliance is up to you. You have to set up and run your own program. It takes longer to do that. If you don't know what you're doing, you risk not being in compliance with the program, and more resources are required because you're not outsourcing compliance or the running of the program to another sponsor.

Option 3: Join an Apprentix-Sponsored Program

Apprentix is also a nationwide Program Sponsor

#3: Join an Apprentix-sponsored program

Pros:

- ✅ Less cost
- ✅ Not alone
- ✅ No unions
- ✅ Customized
- ✅ More control
- ✅ Tech platform
- ✅ No bureaucrats
- ✅ Immediate setup
- ✅ Keep you compliant
- ✅ No pressure to conform

> Apprentix Tech Platform
> +
> Fractional Sponsor™

The third way to establish a registered apprenticeship comes from us at Apprentix. We've invented something unique: we have our own sponsorship, but we operate programs with the understanding that businesses need their programs to be fully customizable and flexible. And because we have a tech platform and we have our own Fractional Sponsor, we can create all the pros without the cons. Our Fractional Sponsor offering is a done-for-you apprenticeship program sponsor service that handles everything from setup and design to registration to ongoing compliance and audits.

With Apprentix's platform and our Fractional Sponsor service, you're part of a program that allows you to keep costs down. You're not alone in all this. There are no unions. You can customize the program completely because we're the ones working to customize it with you onto our platform and monitoring it to make sure that it's working. We have that tech platform. There are no bureaucrats involved here. We set up immediately. We guarantee, for everyone, that their registered apprenticeship program will be set up and launched within thirty days. You can stay compliant because our Fractional Sponsor is responsible for keeping you compliant, and there's no pressure for you to conform because, again, we're operating together. We have no outside government funding that is telling us how we need to behave, and you are simply joining our program.

With the Apprentix platform and our Fractional Sponsor services, you can get a full turnkey apprenticeship program launched and operated at a low cost without all the bureaucratic red tape. If you're interested in getting help with your registered apprenticeship program, if you need to get one set up within thirty days, or if you already have one and you simply want someone to run it and make sure that it stays compliant so that you don't have to keep investing the resources to do that yourself, please contact us. We'll be happy to look at how we can help you. And if you don't need our Fractional Sponsor service because you have everything taken care of in-house but you do want the technology, you can purchase just the technology platform and run your own programs through it.

Now that you know how to get your program registered, it's time to understand what it means to be the program sponsor and admin—two essential functions specific to registered apprenticeships.

Sponsor and Admin Playbook

If you're not looking to create a registered apprenticeship program, you can skip this section, but if you want to understand what a sponsor does that's different from an admin, you'll find this section useful. And if you are starting a registered apprenticeship program, you absolutely must understand what a sponsor does. Whether or not you are going to be the sponsor, you still need to know whether you're going to hire someone external to do this or whether you're going to employ someone yourself.

We're going to start with the roles and responsibilities of the program sponsor, the regulations, and the documentation required. Then we'll dive into the different components of the program sponsor that must be addressed during the registration process, such as the Affirmative Action Plan and the Equal Employment Opportunity Plan.

In term of the roles and responsibilities, we'll cover four topics:

1. Accountability chart
2. What does it take to become a sponsor?
3. What are the sponsor's accountabilities?
4. What are the admin's accountabilities?

1. Accountability Chart

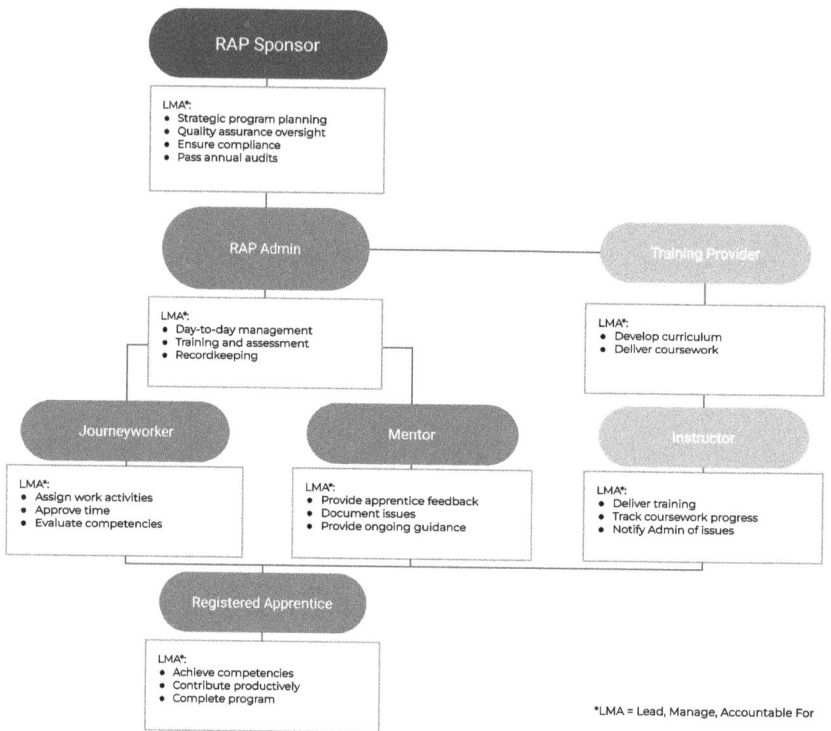

I developed this accountability chart because bureaucrats toss around roles as if the rest of us in business know what the heck they're talking about. By organizing the roles into accountabilities, we see the hierarchy and what each role leads, manages, and is accountable for (LMA).

At the top is the registered apprenticeship program sponsor, also known as the RAP sponsor. The RAP sponsor provides strategic planning for the program itself and quality assurance oversight and ensures compliance while passing annual audits. In contrast, the admin oversees the day-to-day management of the program and manages training, assesses apprentices, evaluates competencies, and ensures records are being kept, evidence is being stored, apprentices are progressing, approvals are being done, and more.

The journeymen complete evaluations, approve time, and assign work to the apprentice. The mentor provides the apprentice with feedback and fosters an understanding of the issues the apprentice might be facing. In addition, the mentor helps the apprentice overcome those issues and then documents what types of feedback and guidance they've provided.

The training provider develops the curriculum and delivers that curriculum. The instructor ensures that training is delivered, that the apprentice's progress is being assessed, and that the admin is being notified of any issues.

Finally, the registered apprentice is responsible simply for becoming competent, being productive, and completing the program.

2. What Does It Take to Become a Sponsor?

To become a sponsor, you must do up to five things:

1. Understand the roles and responsibilities assigned to you as a sponsor.
2. Familiarize yourself with apprenticeship regulations and the guiding documents because the set standards for the sponsor differ from those for the admin.
3. Develop and implement an Affirmative Action Plan. (This is applicable only if you meet certain criteria.)
4. Implement an Equal Employment Opportunity (EEO) Plan and ensure adherence to the plan in the apprentice selection and recruitment process.
5. Register your program with the appropriate governing body, either the OA or the SAA, depending on the state in which the program will operate.

Timeline for Becoming a Program Sponsor

Several factors affect the timeline of becoming a registered apprenticeship program sponsor. The paperwork itself will take a while to fill out because it will probably be new to you. Once you've submitted the final paperwork, assuming you've done it all correctly and completely, it takes about six months to become a sponsor.

The paperwork process can be completely automated through Apprentix, so it'll take you minutes instead of months if you use the platform, but the six-month waiting period is not something Apprentix can help with, unfortunately. That is part of the bureaucracy.

3. What Are the Sponsor's Accountabilities?

In this section, we're going to discuss the five accountabilities of being a program sponsor:

1. Completing the required training

2. Conducting program reviews

3. Recruiting businesses

4. Formulating grievance procedures

5. Reporting compliance

Completing the Required Training

As a program sponsor, you must complete the DoL's EEO training—in addition to creating and implementing an EEO Plan—and training on your state's compliance reporting system. RAPIDS is the centralized database every state uses, so all project sponsors must complete RAPIDS training. Some SAA states also use their own databases and related training. Apprentix automates all these compliance reports. While the training isn't as crucial for Apprentix users, all project sponsors still have to do it, and it's useful to know what needs to be reported, how it should be reported, and how the systems work.

Conducting Program Reviews

A project sponsor must conduct three types of program reviews: performance reviews, quality assurance audits, and safety inspections. We're going to dive into each one of those to make sure that you understand the distinction between the three and the activities that must be performed.

Types of Program Reviews

Performance Reviews

The purpose of a performance review is to assess the effectiveness of the apprenticeship program in terms of training outcomes and apprentice success. The focus areas for a performance review are the apprentice's progression, their completion rates, the quality of their training, and the employment outcomes. What happened when they completed the program? Did they stay with the company? Did they go into this job? Did they go to some other company? In Apprentix, we track where an apprentice goes when they've completed the program and record the reasons for their decision.

The performance review must be led and run by the program sponsor, but it must also include an internal review team, any relevant industry bodies, and any educational partners. Effectively, all those who participate in and influence the program must participate in the performance review so that it includes their input and feedback.

Quality Assurance Audits

Performing quality assurance audits is one of the core functions of a program sponsor, and to assess quality, you must conduct annual performance reviews across all apprentices. The review must define and evaluate factors such as the following:

- Apprentice performance in terms of

  o Start date

  o Coursework progress

  o On-the-job learning progress

  o Comparison to other apprentices in the cohort or to benchmarks

- Bottlenecks within the program that hinder progression

In Apprentix, this is all automated because all activities are tracked and reported.

High Standards of Training and Mentorship

The program sponsor is responsible for ensuring that the apprenticeship program maintains a high standard of training and mentorship. The focus areas here are curriculum events, instructor qualifications, training facilities, equipment, and learning materials. Once again, the program sponsor leads the audit, but any accreditation bodies, industry-specific organizations, educational partners, and people who influence and determine the educational component of the program should participate to evaluate the program and provide feedback.

Collecting Stakeholder Feedback

Stakeholders include apprentices, managers, journey workers, mentors, instructors, and admins. Collecting stakeholder feedback involves identifying relevant feedback topics, initiating feedback collection and collecting feedback, and then incorporating that feedback into program development or updates.

Updating Training Materials

Often, new regulations are issued and industry needs change—due to new technologies, for example. Ensuring that the apprentices are trained on new regulations and skills means that you must update the curriculum and the job-related competencies. Additionally, you should review the strategic partnerships you may have formed to create the apprenticeship program. Perhaps you formed a partnership with a local nonprofit or an education provider. By objectively evaluating their performance, focusing on what they said they would deliver versus what they did to make sure you're getting everything you need, you can ensure that your apprentices are well equipped and able to complete the program.

Safety Inspections

The purpose of safety inspections is to ensure a safe training environment for apprentices. Focus areas are workplace safety, adherence to OSHA standards and regulations, and emergency preparedness. Once again, inspections are led by the sponsor, but the inspections are conducted by OSHA inspectors, state-level safety agencies, or both.

Managing Funding and Resources

As program sponsor, you can find funding and seek out and apply for grants, subsidies, and other funding sources for the program, and you can ensure proper resource allocation and use of those resources. For example, the program might rely on internal resources and different types of people's time, resources from third-party providers, or both. Effective resource management ensures that the right mix of resources is being used and that it's both affordable and effective.

When Do Program Reviews Occur?

The DoL or state governing body schedule and conduct their own program reviews. Typically, a review is conducted at the end of the first year of the program being operational and again after the end of the first full training cycle and at the end of each full training cycle. The reviews will be conducted to ensure that graduates truly have completed the program, the documentation is being retained, and there's evidence that graduates have learned what the program claims to teach. Subsequently, the program will be reviewed at least once every five years.

A review outside the planned review schedule might be conducted if the registration agency receives either credible information of the sponsor's failure to conform to the standards or relevant regulations or a written complaint of a sponsor's failure to conform. For example, if an apprentice claims that they're not learning something they're supposed to be learning, it could trigger an impromptu review by the OA or SAA.

Tools Used for Program Reviews

The DoL and state registration agencies require the use of two tools during program reviews: the Apprenticeship Registration (APR) Tool and Electronic Apprenticeship Progress Record (EAPR) Tool.

APR Tool

The APR Tool contains seven checklist items related to compliance:

1. The program's identifying information

2. The sponsor's details

3. Prior deficiencies or corrections

4. The on-the-job learning plan

5. The classroom plan, also known as related instruction

6. The program's operations procedures

7. The program's selection procedures

EAPR Tool

The EAPR Tool has five compliance-related checklist items that focus on the Affirmative Action Plan:

1. Annual review of the personnel processes

2. Invitations for individuals with disabilities to self-identify

3. Workforce analysis on race, sex, and ethnicity

4. Workforce analysis on disability

5. Targeted outreach that has been done for recruiting and selection activities, if required

Three Components of the Program Review

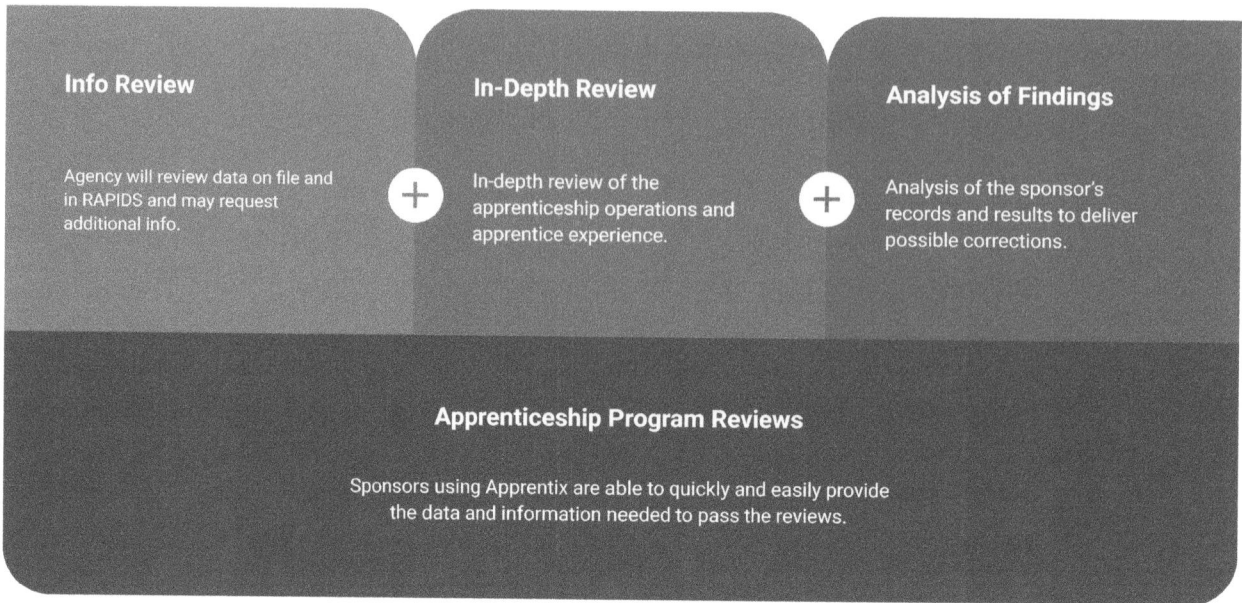

There are three stages to a program review.

Stage 1: Information Review

The agency will review all the data filed in RAPIDS and request additional information not tracked in RAPIDS. Having that information handy greatly simplifies the process, and Apprentix is immensely useful in this regard.

The registration agency will send you, as the program sponsor, a written notice of review that will include the purpose and components of the review, the period the review will cover, the date and time of the actual review, any requests for information and relevant documentation you need to send them, whether the review will be conducted remotely or on site, a reminder to make apprentices and others available for interviews, and the reviewer's name and contact information.

Stage 2: In-Depth Review

During the in-depth review, you will provide the records and data and file the information they need, and the reviewer will review these. Then, the reviewer

- will interview at least one apprentice, maybe more;

- might check the work and training sites;

- will review the demographic information and demographic analysis of the apprentices—if you're using Apprentix, that information will be available in reports, as the platform captures demographic information;

- will review the ratio of journey workers to apprentices; and

- will review the Affirmative Action Plan if applicable.

Stage 3: Analysis of Findings

During this stage, the reviewer will

- report any deficiencies they've identified;

- explain how to remedy them, if applicable;

- indicate when you have to do that by; and

- describe the enforcement actions that may be undertaken if compliance is not achieved within the time frame given.

Responding to the Program Review

You can either accept the reviewer's findings or submit a written rebuttal to the findings. If you agree with the findings and remedies, you must submit a compliance action plan that must include the following components:

- A written commitment to take action

- Precise, named actions

- The time required to make these changes

- The primary point of contact

The alternative entails disagreeing with any of the findings, remedies, or both and submitting a written rebuttal. The registration agency will determine one of three possible outcomes, which will be documented as shown in the following table:

	Option #1	Option #2	Option #3
Registration Agency's Decision	Agrees with all rebutted items	Agrees to some rebutted items	Upholds the original Notice of Findings with no changes
Registration Agency's Recommendation	Amended	Amended	Upheld
Written Notice	New Notice of Findings	Amended Notice of Findings after sponsor submits compliance action plan	Notice: Compliance action plan due
Findings Within the Notice	No findings of deficiency	Findings for the areas identified	Uphold original findings

1. The agency can agree with your rebuttals, in which case they'll amend their recommendations and issue a notice that no deficiencies need to be corrected.

2. The agency can agree with some of the rebutted items and amend the recommendations and submit a new filing. You'll have to respond to that filing because it will contain items that they refuted and that they agreed with. You'll have to deal with the things they refuted, either by providing a plan or lodging another rebuttal.

3. The agency can uphold the original findings and not agree with you at all. If they uphold them, you'll need to submit the compliance action plan and address the deficiencies or lodge another rebuttal.

Conducting Outreach and Advocacy

The program sponsor is also responsible for outreach and advocacy. This is important for promoting the program itself, which in turn helps you attract potential apprentices and, potentially, more funding. And because program sponsors can work with multiple employers, you may also be looking to attract other employers. Now, would you work with your competitors? Probably not, but you might be working with other types of companies that need the same apprenticeship program. Although it is rare, if that's the case, you'll also want to attract other employers.

In terms of advocacy, you want to be able to engage stakeholders. That might mean updating stakeholders by contacting them and letting them know what's going on. It also gives you the opportunity to gather their feedback and updates.

OA Standards for National Programs

If you do find yourself in a situation where you have to recruit businesses, you're required to build out an employer network and assign three initial employers as part of your sponsored program. This means you'll have to include some competitors, which is unusual, or at least companies that might not be competitors but that need the exact thing you have. You'll also have to sign a declaration of future expansion that includes potential employers and locations. With this declaration, you swear that you're going to try to expand the program and enroll other businesses, and you specify what that target looks like.

SAA Standards for One-State Programs

SAA agencies have standards for one-state programs that require sponsors to sign just one initial employer. These programs are specific to only one state. Once a program is set up, you can be added into that RAPIDS database.

Formulating Grievance Procedures

Program sponsors are also responsible for formulating grievance procedures. The purpose of a grievance procedure is to clearly state that you are emphasizing and ensuring the fairness of and addressing concerns with the apprenticeship program. Define what types of issues or concerns are covered under the grievance procedure, thinking through all the things that might come up and the processes for how you'll handle them. This doesn't mean you must have a solution for how you're going to handle each issue; instead, identify the process for how you're going to handle it.

Resolution Attempts

There must be an informal resolution attempt. For a grievance procedure, encourage apprentices to first attempt to solve or resolve the issue on their own by discussing it either directly with the party involved or with their immediate supervisor. Rather than escalating the issue to the sponsor as a grievance, encourage apprentices to handle it on their own. You can help them set a reasonable time limit for this step, typically five to seven business days, so that they can resolve it quickly and fairly without engaging you formally as a sponsor.

But if that doesn't work, they do have to have the ability to submit a formal grievance, so you need to have a procedure for that too. If the issue isn't resolved, the apprentice must submit the grievance in writing. It must be in writing and cannot just be reported verbally. The grievance should clearly describe the issue, the parties involved, any attempts at informal resolution, and the desired outcome. Provide information on how to submit the grievance—where and to whom.

Grievance Review Process

You must acknowledge receipt of the grievance within a specified time, such as three business days. Then, assign an impartial reviewer or a committee to investigate the grievance. This may involve interviewing relevant parties, reviewing documents, and gathering facts. Set a reasonable and specific time frame for the review process— typically five to fifteen business days.

Resolution and Response

After the review, the person or committee responsible for handling the grievance should make the decision. They must provide a written response to the apprentice explaining the decision and the rationale behind it within a specific time frame, such as within five business days of completing the review.

Appeal Process

If the apprentice is not satisfied with the decision, they should be able to appeal. Outline the appeals process—describe how to submit the appeal and to whom. Detail the process for the final review of the appeal, which should be conducted by a different person or committee than the initial review.

Recordkeeping

Keep all records of grievances, investigations, and resolutions. If you're using Apprentix, you can upload those records into the document storage area.

Nonretaliation Clause

Ensure that all the proceedings are confidential to protect the privacy of those involved. Include a nonretaliation clause in the policy that clearly states that an apprentice who files a grievance or participates in a grievance procedure will be protected from any retaliation.

Regular Review of Grievance Procedure

Review the grievance procedure regularly and conduct a periodic review to ensure that it remains effective and in compliance with any changes to laws and regulations.

Distribution and Accessibility

Distribute the grievance policy so that all apprentices and staff are aware of the grievance procedure. Additionally, make it easy to access in case somebody needs to refer to it—for example, by including it in the employee or program handbook or any type of training. It's a good idea to also include this in the apprentice training itself as part of the classroom instruction. Make the grievance procedure, or all the procedures that they need to know, one of the courses they need to spend time on so that they not only have been provided access to it but also have spent the hours to have taken the course to learn it. It will give them extra comfort that they surely do know what the grievance procedure is.

Reporting Compliance

The project sponsor is responsible for reporting compliance. But compliance is "do this or else," so let's walk through the "what you need to do or else."

Compliance Requirement	Who to Report To	Frequency	Reporting System
Adherence to Apprenticeship Standards	Federal/state agencies	Annually	RAPIDS
Equal Employment Opportunity (EEO) Compliance	DoL	Annually	EEO Reporting System
Wage & Hour Law Compliance	DoL	Annually	Wage Reporting System
Health & Safety Standards	Occupational Safety and Health Administration (OSHA)	As required	OSHA Reporting System
Recordkeeping & Reporting	State/federal agencies	Quarterly/ annually	RAPIDS

Labor Laws & Regulations	DoL	Annually	Labor Law Reporting System
Accessibility & Accommodations	DoL	As required	ADA Compliance System
Quality Assurance	Internal/external auditors	Annually	Internal reporting
Apprenticeship Certification	DoL	Upon completion	RAPIDS
Industry-Specific Regulations	Relevant industry bodies	As required	Industry-specific systems
Insurance & Liability	Insurance providers	Annually	Internal/provider reporting
Partnership & Collaboration	Partners/legal departments	As required	Internal reporting

Adherence to Apprenticeship Standards

You need to adhere to the apprenticeship standards, whether the federal and state regulations or the program standards you've set. Basically, what did you say you were going to do? Are you doing it? That's the umbrella statement around adherence to the apprenticeship standards.

Equal Employment Opportunity (EEO) Compliance

Make sure your plan is in place, that it has all the elements we described, that the plan is being followed, and that there isn't any type of discrimination occurring. That's the other piece of compliance strictly around EEO.

Wage and Hour Law Compliance

The Fair Labor Standards Act sets out compliance with minimum wage and overtime provisions. You also have the progressive wage schedule that is being implemented. You've determined the starting wage, wage progressions, and the completion wage, all while tracking each wage change.

No one's ever going to penalize you for paying more, so if your wage progressions say one thing and you've been paying more all along, no one's going to question that. Problems arise only if you pay less or if you don't pay on time.

Health and Safety Standards

These include complying with OSHA standards and conducting safety training to make sure apprentices are safe and healthy at work.

Recordkeeping and Reporting

Part of compliance is recordkeeping and reporting. You have to maintain detailed records of apprentices' progress and not just a payroll that records how many hours they worked. Instead, records should show how they spent their working hours, what their wages are, and program completion rates. Reporting includes submitting regular reports to the relevant state or federal agency.

Labor Laws and Regulations

You have to have apprenticeship agreements in place and comply with labor laws, including child labor, harassment, and workplace discrimination laws.

Accessibility and Accommodations

Part of compliance is accessibility and accommodations as per the Americans with Disabilities Act, ensuring accessibility for apprentices with disabilities and providing them with reasonable accommodations as needed.

Quality Assurance

Quality assurance relates to program reviews and audits, continuous improvements to collect feedback, and using that feedback to improve your program.

Apprenticeship Certification

When an apprentice completes their apprenticeship program, you must submit an Application of Certificate of Completion to the DoL. Make sure that they receive their certificate.

Industry-Specific Regulations

Ensure compliance with any industry-specific regulations, specifically those related to health care, construction, and electrical occupations. Those industries have their own training and certification requirements, so make sure that you're in compliance with those.

Insurance and Liability

Make sure that you have enough insurance and liability coverage.

Partnership and Collaboration

If you have any types of agreements with partners or any collaborations, have those reviewed, and make sure that they are legally documented and that you are all doing the job you said you would do according to those agreements.

4. What Are the Admin's Accountabilities?

Operational Management Responsibilities

The admin's accountabilities differ from those of the project sponsor. The admin's focus is on operational management responsibilities, which means they must track all the records of each apprentice, including maintaining and updating those records. This includes progress: What courses has the apprentice taken? What courses have they not taken? How much time have they tracked? What competency evaluations have been performed on them? What type of assessments have been done on them? In which competencies have they been rated proficient? Where are they still in training? Where are they not in training? What is coming up in terms of wage progressions? What wage progressions are they eligible for? Many, many factors are involved in the day-to-day program operations, and those are the pieces of recordkeeping that must be tracked and stored.

Simple scheduling also falls under operational management. This involves making sure that

- apprentices are being trained,
- their schedules are being updated,
- their supervisors or mentors are on the job with them to be able to train them, and
- examinations and assessments are taking place.

Communication and Support

Admins also provide communication and support, so they tend to be liaisons and act as the primary point of contact for apprentices, trainers, and sponsors. In some cases, they might be working and sharing information with sponsors informally. For example, those who use Apprentix's Fractional Sponsor service have access to an exclusive private community of sponsors of other programs and like-minded folks who they can share knowledge with and gain knowledge from.

Problem Solving

Apprentices, trainers, or journey workers might raise concerns or have complaints. The admin tends to be the first point of contact before potentially escalating the matter to the sponsor, if needed.

Compliance and Reporting

The admin must regularly monitor activities to make sure the program stays compliant. This is easily done in Apprentix, where clear, complete reports can be generated at the touch of a button. The reports contain data that shows how everyone is performing against the standards they're supposed to be meeting.

Monthly reporting typically includes reports from apprentices and managers that contain data that must be monitored and measured to ensure that apprentices are progressing. This can include reports on time tracking and approval, evaluation requests, and completed evaluations.

Managing Training and Assessment

In terms of training, admins must manage all the logistics of the training sessions. Whether the training is conducted in person, on site, or at a community college, the program admin must make sure the time is blocked off, the room is booked, the instructors attend (so if somebody is off sick, there's a backup involved), and the relevant materials and equipment are available and operational. Quite a bit goes into just the classroom aspect.

Additionally, admins oversee the assessments to ensure that the assessments and evaluations are being designed and performed and that, for example, managers know how to assess the apprentices properly and how to conduct performance or skills evaluations.

Admins also gather feedback and collect information, possibly through surveys or one-on-one conversations or both. They might implement this feedback in the day-to-day operations of the program to improve the program. This process might not necessarily change the overall structure of the program or need to be communicated to the program sponsor. For example, someone might say that it would be helpful to have the machines the apprentices are learning about in the classroom so that they can see what they're learning about. This type of day-to-day issue wouldn't structurally change what the sponsor does.

Administrative Duties

Lastly, admins are responsible for administrative duties around documentation and recordkeeping—making sure that everything's up to date and accurate. When an audit is carried out, the data must exist, preferably at the push of a button (which is the case in Apprentix). Without the data, the program will fail the audit and there could be confusion about who has done what, who has approved what, what evidence exists, and so on.

Of course, on the budget side, admins need to identify potential budget overruns and areas where budget increases are needed to facilitate activities. Admins should take a tactical approach and ask, "What are we funding, and what should we be funding?" to ensure that resources are being allocated effectively.

Now, I know it sounds like there's some overlap between the program sponsor and the admin. Generally, they are distinct, but they do have similar functions at different levels. Let's walk through what those key differences are to make sure that they're explicitly clear.

What Are the Key Differences between the Accountabilities of the Program Sponsor and Admin?

The key differences between the accountabilities of program sponsors and admins relate to their scopes of responsibility. Sponsors operate at a broader strategic level. They make sure the program is set up and the apprenticeship's framework is designed in the right way. They ensure the compliance of that framework with standards and regulations, and they find any funding if needed. In contrast, admins are involved in the operational aspects of the program.

On the interaction level, sponsors are removed from daily activities, whereas admins are the point of contact for people on a day-to-day basis. From a decision-making standpoint, sponsors look at things from a strategic level and make decisions, and then they delegate those decisions to the admins. The admins operationalize or implement the decisions into the programs.

Apprenticeship Regulations and Guiding Documents

Now we're going to move on to apprenticeship regulations and guiding documents. Let's start by looking at regulations at the federal level.

Federal Regulations

On the federal level, the following acts and regulations apply to apprenticeship programs:

- The **Fair Labor Standards Act** (FLSA) covers minimum wage, overtime pay, and child labor laws. This is no different than for all other employees. Apprentices may be subject to special provisions under the FLSA.

- The **Equal Employment Opportunity** (EEO) Commission regulations must be followed for all apprenticeship programs. Apprenticeship programs must be accessible and provide equal employment opportunities regardless of race, ethnicity, religion, national origin, age, disability, and genetic information. Effectively, don't discriminate.

- **OSHA regulations** govern the provision of a safe and healthy work environment for apprentices. You must obviously meet any OSHA regulations.

- The **Americans with Disabilities Act** (ADA) ensures that accommodations are made for apprentices with disabilities if you're hiring them.

- The **National Apprenticeship Act**, known as the Fitzgerald Act, which was passed in 1937, effectively governs the apprenticeship program itself—all the registration requirements, the operation, and the certification. You must understand all that, which is what I've been teaching you here.

At the federal level, it's pretty much business as usual, other than EEO requirements and adhering to the regulations in the National Apprenticeship Act.

State-Level Regulations

At the state level, the *Chevron* deference has allowed state agencies to interpret federal laws to provide more clarity. On June 28, 2024, the Supreme Court overturned this, and as of now, each state has interpreted the federal regulations in the previous section and implemented them how they see fit. As a result, we have an inconsistent system that varies from state to state in its requirements and preferences. Here are some regulations you need to know about as well:

- State apprenticeship requirements regarding wages, hours, and work conditions, which vary state by state.
- State DoL requirements that often involve registration with their department and compliance with state-specific labor laws.
- Industry-specific regulations—certain industries, such as construction, health care, and electrical, may have additional state-specific training and certification requirements that you have to comply with.

You'll have to contact the apprenticeship office within each state you want to register to learn their requirements.

Program-Specific Regulations and Documentation

Apprenticeship Standards

You must document and store the standards of apprenticeship. Standards are the outline of the program structure, including the coursework, on-the-job training, and details about the apprenticeship program. They also outline what competency requirements and benchmarks must exist for apprentices, the duration of the apprenticeship program, and the criteria the apprentice must meet to progress.

For example, how long will the program be? Who will provide the training? What certificate will be earned? Effectively, you're saying, "Here's the plan, and we're going to meet the plan."

Apprenticeship Agreements

An apprenticeship agreement is the agreement between the apprentice and the sponsor that details the responsibilities and expectations of each party. The agreement includes all the terms in the apprenticeship standards. By signing the agreement, the apprentice is saying, "I know and acknowledge that this is what I'm going to be going through." Apprenticeship agreements are signed by both parties and stored. You must complete these forms in a specific way and update RAPIDS.

Pro Tip: Apprentix Automates Standards and Apprenticeship Agreements

One of the beauties of Apprentix is that it walks you through all the standards of apprenticeship within the platform. Once you answer plain-English questions, all the standards will generate automatically for you.

Apprentix also generates apprenticeship agreements completely filled out for you, and you can digitally sign and store them within the platform.

Wage Progressions

The next program-specific regulation is wage skills, also known as wage progressions. It effectively establishes what an apprentice is going to earn when they start, what they're going to earn when they complete the program, and at least one wage bump along the way. Often, a registered apprenticeship includes multiple wage bumps to motivate apprentices to move on, and you must be able to document when those wage bumps will be implemented.

Wage and Hour Records

You want to have documentation of the apprentice's wages, their wage bumps, and any benefits that have been provided. And you want to make sure that the wages that have been paid comply with the Fair Labor Standards Act and any local wage laws. You can draw this data from your payroll system.

Recordkeeping

Recordkeeping requires you to store the apprentice's hours, competencies, and training, and you must report on this regularly through a centralized database. OA states all use the RAPIDS database. In SAA states, some use RAPIDS and some use their own databases, but they all do report into RAPIDS.

> **Pro Tip: Apprentix Automates Compliance Reporting**
>
> In Apprentix, you can click a button and download an automatically generated report that you can import into RAPIDS directly, so it automates RAPIDS compliance reporting.

Quality Assurance

Quality assurance refers to performing program audits and ensuring that the program is meeting the quality standards you've set out for and that training is happening how it should.

Grant Reporting

If you receive grant funding, you'll likely need to submit a report into the Workforce Integrated Performance System, known as WIPS. Let's say you were to receive funding from the Workforce Innovation and Opportunity Act (WIOA). You'd have to comply with regulations and performance reporting measures. In fact, if you ever receive any type of funding, there will always be some strings attached. They're not just going to give you money for nothing. You'd have to adhere to whatever those compliance and reporting needs are.

Insurance and Liability

Apprentices are employees, so you'll already have liability coverage for them. There might be some issues that you need to bring up with your insurance provider specific to an apprentice to see if it distinguishes between the liability coverage for an apprentice and a standard employee. Typically, that won't be the case, but confirm this to make sure that your apprentices are adequately covered too. Also make sure that the documentation is stored with the coverage amounts so that you know apprentices have been covered.

Safety and Health Training Records

You also must maintain safety and health training records, so document the safety training that's been provided along with OSHA standards, if that's applicable to your occupation. You must also have any records of health and safety certifications that are required of the program.

You can store all these in Apprentix, but you do need to keep them handy in case of an audit or so that when the audit happens, you've got everything really buttoned up.

Registration Documents

Registration forms, whether federal or in an OA or SAA state, need to be filled out in a specific way. One of the things I wanted to do when I built Apprentix was remove all this bureaucracy, all the red tape, all the issues that arise if you don't know how to fill out a form or if you fill out a form incorrectly, given every state has their own people who run it with their own preferences. We've automated all of that in Apprentix to cut through all that red tape.

If you do this on your own, you have to make sure you don't mess this up. It's not the most complicated thing in the world, but when you're not familiar with the language and you make a mistake, you end up in an exception pile, and exception piles within the government are no place to live. You want to be in the pile that's fully conformed to what they need. And, fortunately, Apprentix will take care of that for you.

> **Pro Tip: Apprentix Automatically Completes Registration Documents**
>
> In Apprentix, you can automatically generate the registration forms by letting the system know that you'd like to start a new apprenticeship program and selecting the state where your program will be located. With the click of a button, Apprentix will complete the forms for you so you don't have to worry about learning legalese or making a mistake.

EEO Plan

In the EEO Plan, you have to document what that EEO Plan is, including the outline, and set out the sponsor's commitment to not discriminate. This includes how you're going to recruit, select, train, and employ your apprentices.

> **Pro Tip: Apprentix Automatically Generates an EEO Plan**
>
> The EEO Plan is automatically generated for you. Simply review it and sign off on it, and it will be stored within the Signed Documents section of Apprentix.

Progress Reports

Progress reports include regular assessments of each apprentice's skills and knowledge development and any evaluations from their supervisors or mentors.

Pro Tip: Apprentix Has Views and Reports to Make Progress Reporting Easy

You can monitor the progress of any individual apprentice, cohort of apprentices, or all apprentices within a program. You can view performance within the platform itself and generate reports that show you progress in a clean format that's easy to share.

Attendance Records

Attendance records show when apprentices logged time, what day, and how many hours they spent on what course or what competency. This is very different from payroll. Payroll indicates only that a person was at work on a particular day and worked so many hours, and it pays them for those hours.

Completion and Certification Records

Attendance records are related to completion and certification records, as apprentices must record what they spent their working hours on. Again, this is not something covered by payroll systems. Once an apprentice has completed the hours required for the program, as evidenced by their attendance record, you must document that they have completed the program and certify their completion, and then you must report that completion.

Likewise, if somebody is dismissed from the program because they simply didn't finish, they quit or were fired, or they took a leave of absence, you must document that and update the RAPIDS database. Again, Apprentix will automate this for you, but you must know that these are all aspects of the requirements that you must fulfill.

Pro Tip: Generate Request for Certification Forms

When an apprentice completes their program, you can click a button to automatically create the forms needed to request a Certificate of Apprenticeship Completion.

Competency Evaluations

Competency evaluations assess whether an apprentice is not in training, in training, or proficient with a particular skill. A manager evaluates an apprentice's competency and documents evidence so that it's clear who evaluated the apprentice, when, and why they rated the apprentice in the way they did on that date. In Apprentix, you can create competency evaluations and apprentices can request to be evaluated—a great way for them to take ownership of their own progress.

Feedback

Feedback is often provided by a mentor directly to the apprentice, but it can be provided by anyone working with that apprentice. Feedback can also be documented *about* the apprentice, and when this feedback isn't shared with the apprentice, it's known as case management or private notes.

Assessments

You can create assessments related to apprentices using questions and answers that you want people to answer about the apprentices. These templated assessments are helpful when regular check-ins need to be performed. Examples of assessments you may create are Wage Increase Eligible, 90-Day Probationary Period, Year 1, and so on.

Pro Tip: Create Custom Assessments in Apprentix

You can create custom assessments with your own questions and answer choices. The uses for assessments are unlimited, and customers use them to assess managers, mentors, and apprentices across various milestones, such as the end of a probationary period, and for performance evaluation, wage increases, and more.

Audit and Compliance Reports

At some point, you will be audited. The audit process can be complex, but in simple terms, you'll have to review the audit findings and provide the details that justify the auditor's queries and remedy any issues there may be. Fortunately, Apprentix makes this super easy because everything needed in an audit is documented on the platform. But if you're not using Apprentix, make sure that you have all the audit and compliance trails well documented and stored and easily accessible. You don't want to be running around trying to find people's spreadsheets and papers that they've filled out on the job site. That is one guaranteed way of failing an audit and burning everyone out, so you don't want to be in that business.

Partnership Agreements (If Applicable)

If you're working with any partner, such as an educational institution, an industry partner like an association, or any other stakeholder, it's important that you have that partnership agreement stored and saved so that you know the scope of that agreement. That could be a partnership agreement or something as simple as a memorandum of understanding. Whatever it is, make sure the roles are well defined—what they're supposed to do, what you're supposed to receive, and what you're supposed to do.

Grant or Funding Documentation (If Applicable)

If you receive any grants or any type of funding at all, keep the documentation. Know what you're supposed to store in terms of documents, what type of reporting you're supposed to provide, and any type of agreements that you're supposed to sign. Keep it all in one easy-to-access place.

Pro Tip: Document Storage in Apprentix

You can upload documents and store them in Apprentix. This is handy—you can keep all the relevant signed paperwork in one place.

The Registration Process

Now let's look at the registration process itself. We'll review five key components:

1. Developing an Equal Employment Opportunity (EEO) Plan

2. Developing an Affirmative Action Plan

3. Registering the program

4. Registering the occupations

Separating the registration of the program and occupations isn't an error—those are two different actions that must be completed separately.

Developing an Equal Employment Opportunity Plan

Purpose of an EEO Plan

The purpose of an EEO Plan is to prevent discrimination—bottom line. It's to ensure that your hiring, screening, selection, and training processes are fair and that everyone has a fair chance at getting the job.

Applicability

Who must do this? You.

If you run a registered apprenticeship program, you absolutely must do this. I'm not sure why it's highlighted for registered apprenticeship programs because the law applies to any hiring. You also have to document that you have an EEO Plan. Fortunately, Apprentix will do that for you.

Components of an EEO Plan

What must go into the EEO Plan? If you're using Apprentix, the platform automatically generates the EEO Plan for you. If not, you must include several components:

- An explicit clause on nondiscrimination, a clear policy, and a declared commitment to the prohibition of discrimination.

- A designated EEO officer. This requirement doesn't necessarily exist in the general law but is needed for a registered apprenticeship. Is that a separate person from the sponsor or admin? No, it's simply the name of the person responsible for ensuring that there is a plan and that the plan follows the guidelines set out in this section.

- Complaint procedures. You must establish a process for an apprentice to file a discrimination complaint. This section must include who to complain to, the investigation process, and how complaints are dealt with (i.e., the resolution protocols). In Apprentix, you can assign a person who deals with complaints, and then complaints are automatically routed to them.

- It is crucial that complaints are documented and followed up on. The complaint procedure must be well documented, from complaint initiation to the investigation to the resolution.

- A plan for regular training for staff and apprentices on the EEO policies. That can be something as simple as a reminder with the EEO Plan attached to something as formal as training. You can choose the path, but you do need to lay out what the training program will be, and then you need to follow it.

- A strategy to recruit a diverse pool of candidates. Now, you might be thinking, "What does that matter? I'm just going to find the best person for the job." Agreed, you are. What they're trying to do is get you to open up the top of the funnel. You will select people from the top of the funnel based on your business's needs, but the top of the funnel needs to be filled with as many people from underrepresented classes as possible.

- How are you going to do that? That is a big question. Apprentix includes a database of 139 alternative recruiting sources that you can draw on to find people to satisfy this requirement, but you do need a documented plan for attracting a diverse pool of candidates into the top of the funnel.

- Selection criteria. You need to document the selection process and ensure that it doesn't lead to discrimination. The selection criteria you list shouldn't contain any type of bias or discrimination.

- A clause that expressly states that you will provide reasonable accommodations to any individuals with disabilities or any type of special needs. *Special needs* is a vague term, so you might want to consult your HR or labor attorney on this policy. Alternatively, you can include specific language around it (e.g., "We make our best efforts to provide reasonable accommodations to anyone with disabilities or other needs") and then handle accommodations on a case-by-case basis. However, the plan must be documented.

You must disseminate the EEO plan to all participants, including the apprentices and staff, to make sure everyone is aware of the EEO policy. It can't just live on a drive somewhere—it must be shared and included in new starts' welcome packages or onboarding training. Finally, you must document and store any type of EEO efforts, complaints, training, resolutions, and investigations. All activities around this must be documented and stored.

Compliance and Enforcement

When it comes to EEO plans, you also must ensure compliance with and enforcement of the plan. Thus, you have to have regular reviews and audits to periodically assess the program's adherence to those policies and practices. You must make sure that you're in compliance with legal standards, that the federal, state, and local EEO requirements are being met, and that any corrective actions are being implemented in the case of noncompliance or any findings of discrimination.

Legal and Ethical Considerations

Legal and ethical considerations include adherence to relevant laws, ethical practices in the treatment of all apprentices and staff, transparency and accountability, and continuous improvement. The relevant laws include the Civil Rights Act, the Americans with Disabilities Act, and the Age Discrimination in Employment Act, which is no different from the laws that apply to regular employees. Transparency and accountability apply not only to the program itself but also to apprentices, who should be following EEO practices and be held accountable for the performance of the EEO Plan. Hiring and training must also adhere to the EEO Plan. Finally, you must continue to improve the EEO Plan and its enforcement based on changes to laws and new guidance that's issued.

Developing an Affirmative Action Plan

Although Affirmative Action Plans and EEO Plans are viewed as the same in some industries, they differ in the context of registered apprenticeships.

Purpose of an Affirmative Action Plan

An Affirmative Action Plan as it relates to apprenticeships ensures equal opportunities in the recruitment, selection, and training of apprentices and trying to include people of underrepresented classes, such as minorities, women, individuals with disabilities, and veterans, and bring them into your recruiting process. I know this is identical to the EEO Plan, but you still need to have this documented as a separate plan. I don't know why, but that's how it goes.

Applicability

Although everyone needs an EEO Plan, not everyone needs an Affirmative Action Plan. If you meet the following criteria, you need an Affirmative Action Plan in addition to an EEO Plan:

- You are a sponsor working with **five or more apprentices**.
- Your program works **directly with federal contracts** such as the Inflation Reduction Act.

If you are required to have an Affirmative Action Plan, make sure that it's separate from the EEO Plan and that it's titled as such.

Components of an Affirmative Action Plan

While the general purpose of an Affirmative Action Plan is identical to that of an EEO Plan, the components are a little different:

- Utilization analysis. This is an assessment of the current workforce and apprenticeship participants conducted by the program sponsor to identify areas where certain groups may be underrepresented. The assessment involves a macroeconomic view of the workforce in general in the geographic area in which the program is operating and the occupations included in it to see who's underrepresented.

- Goals and timetables. You must set specific and measurable goals with clear timelines to improve the representation of underrepresented groups. If you're going to do any type of outreach or post jobs in specific places, you must have deadlines for when you'll do that, and then you must show that you did it.

- Recruitment and outreach strategies. You might work with partners on this to identify some apprentices. Sometimes, you can approach, for example, community organizations that create pre-apprenticeship programs designed specifically for your occupation and from which it would make sense to funnel apprentices into your program. Pre-apprenticeships are simply short training programs that prepare participants for apprenticeships by teaching them a little about the jobs they're interested in. They're not real apprenticeships because the participants don't have jobs, but they are useful for vetting people and a good source of candidates who should like the job and want to progress and end up in your apprenticeship program. You can even approach schools. Whatever you decide, you must define your recruitment and outreach strategies and then develop these strategies to make sure that they include underrepresented groups.

- Nondiscriminatory, fair, unbiased, and transparent selection procedures, like in the EEO Plan. You should include an internal audit procedure to ensure that the plan is effective and that you're adjusting it as necessary.

Finally, you're responsible for making sure that people are assigned within the organization to monitor the plan and make sure that it's implemented correctly. All people involved with this policy must be named, trained, and adhering to the regulation itself, and you must make sure that all that's documented.

Compliance and Enforcement

In terms of compliance and enforcement, ensure that there are regular reviews and updates and that the documentation is maintained for that. If you need to report progress and compliance to regulatory agencies (e.g., the OA, SAA, or DoL), make sure that's being done, and work with these agencies on issues you need advice or guidance on.

Legal and Ethical Considerations

Like the EEO Plan, the Affirmative Action Plan must comply with all relevant nondiscrimination, employment, and other laws. I suggest that you avoid quotas. The plan is not to be misconstrued as having quotas. In registered apprenticeship programs, Affirmative Action Plans do not have any quotas whatsoever. This is all about the intent to try to recruit and select and train people from diverse backgrounds. Ultimately, you must hire people based on merit—who you think is best for the job.

Register Your Program with an OA or SAA state

OA States
1. Alaska
2. Arkansas
3. American Samoa
4. California
5. Georgia
6. Iowa
7. Idaho
8. Illinois
9. Indiana
10. Michigan
11. Missouri
12. Northern Mariana Islands
13. Mississippi
14. North Dakota
15. Nebraska
16. New Hampshire
17. New Jersey
18. Oklahoma
19. Puerto Rico
20. South Carolina
21. South Dakota
22. Texas
23. Utah
24. West Virginia
25. Wyoming

Element	OA State	SAA State
Develop Program Standards	✓	✓
Complete Federal Registration Form	✓	
Submit Standards and Forms to OA	✓	
OA Review and Approval	✓	
Receive Certificate of Registration from OA	✓	
Contact State Agency		✓
Complete State-Specific Forms		✓
Submit Documentation to SAA		✓
SAA Review and Approval		✓
Receive State Certification		✓
Employer Identification Number (EIN)	✓	✓
Equal Employment Opportunity (EEO) Plan	✓	✓
Safety and Health Plans	✓	✓
Detailed Training Outline	✓	✓
Wage Progression Schedule	✓	✓
Collaboration with Educational Institutions	✓	✓
Consultation with Legal or Industry Experts	✓	✓
Regular Updates	✓	✓

SAA States
1. Alabama
2. Arizona
3. California
4. Colorado
5. Connecticut
6. District of Columbia
7. Delaware
8. Florida
9. Guam
10. Hawaii
11. Kansas
12. Kentucky
13. Louisiana
14. Massachusetts
15. Maryland
16. Maine
17. Minnesota
18. Montana
19. North Carolina
20. New Mexico
21. Nevada
22. New York
23. Ohio
24. Oregon
25. Pennsylvania
26. Rhode Island
27. Tennessee
28. Virginia
29. Virgin Islands
30. Vermont
31. Washington
32. Wisconsin

As shown in the above chart, the program registration process differs in OA and SAA states. While some elements of the application overlap, several steps apply only to OA states and several only to SAA states. Because the elements of the registration process are discussed in detail in various sections of this book, I'm not going to discuss them again. However, the chart provides granular details that you can use as a guide to see what you need to do and submit in the state or states in which you want to register your apprenticeship program.

Registering an Apprenticeship Occupation

In addition to registering the apprenticeship program, you must register the occupations included in the program. I've discussed some of the steps below in earlier chapters, so if you've started to work on your program, you should have most of the necessary information in hand.

Step 1: Identify the Occupation

Determine the occupation in which you want to create the apprenticeship. This occupation must be a recognized trade or profession with a clear set of skills or competencies, and it must appear on the DoL's "Apprenticeable Occupations" list, which is available online. The list is a database that is supposed to be kept up to date so that users can access information in real time. However, this isn't always the case.

If you don't see the occupation you want to apprentice on the list, check for close matches. If the job title and summary are a close match, you may need to adjust your terminology. If you still don't see a match, contact your state governing body for a further evaluation of whether the occupation you want to register is an apprenticeable occupation or not. If you're using Apprentix, simply search the job title or the occupation title to find it.

Step 2: Develop a Work Process Schedule

The work process schedule is an outline of all the skills, processes, and competencies an apprentice will learn during their training, and it should include the approximate amount of time that needs to be spent on each part of the training. For example, if an apprentice will learn how to hang drywall, and that will take forty hours, you must outline the skill and include the time required to master it. This will allow the apprentice to track their forty hours toward completion.

Apprentix automatically generates work process schedule outlines based on apprenticeable occupations, and then it allows you to add custom competencies. You can customize the outlines and add the hours required for each competency so that your apprentices can track their time against those competencies.

Step 3: Establish Related Instructional Curriculum

The curriculum is known as the related curriculum, related instructional curriculum, or related technical instructional (RTI) curriculum. This simply refers to the classes the apprentices will take. You must outline the classes, what apprentices are supposed to learn, and how many hours are required per class.

Step 4: Determine the Training Approach and Duration

All registered apprenticeships must be at least one year long, or two thousand hours, but if the apprenticeship is longer, you must spell out how much longer. You must also indicate the training approach (discussed in detail in Section III, "Training Approaches"):

- time based—completion is based on the number of hours the apprentice completed (minimum of two thousand hours for the program),
- competency based—completion is based on whether the apprentice is proficient (after a minimum of two thousand hours for the program), or
- hybrid—completion is based on a combination of competency and time spent.

The hybrid approach is useful when you want to require an apprentice to work a minimum number of hours on a competency before you evaluate whether they can do it or not. If the apprentice isn't proficient yet, you don't sign off on the competency until you observe that they can perform the actual work.

Step 5: Set the Wage Scale

The wage scale includes the starting wage, increases, and the completion wage, as discussed in Section III, "Wage Bump Builder." This should include what the wage progressions are based on—hours, course completions, competency completions, interim credentials earned, or something else—and increases as dollar amounts or percentages.

Step 6: Draft an Apprenticeship Agreement

The apprenticeship agreement should reflect all the apprenticeship components so that when an apprentice reviews it and signs it, they know exactly what they're agreeing to.

Step 7: Submit the Documentation to the Apprenticeship Agency

The next step in registering an apprenticeship occupation is to submit the apprenticeship agreement and accompanying documentation required by the agency, whether it's an OA state or an SAA state. The documentation will include the standards of apprenticeship (i.e., the outline of the program structure, including the coursework, on-the-job training, and details about the apprenticeship program) and an Appendix A, which is part of the registration packet.

In Apprentix, all these forms are automated, so it's much simpler. However, it's still important to know what documents the state requires you to submit.

Step 8: Agency Review

The agency will review your documentation and either request revisions or more information or approve it. In Apprentix, you can send the application pack to the state, and we have a 100 percent acceptance rate because applications completed in Apprentix are complete.

Although the process should be uniform in OA states, the people who run individual offices and oversee reviewing the paperwork have their own preferences. They might tweak minor things just because they like them a certain way. No one can prevent this because it is dependent on who is in the job, and there isn't a requirement for them to stop doing that. The only requirement is to use the form as it is. The good news is that if you're generating the forms out of Apprentix, your application will be accepted because all the information is complete. The reviewers might simply tweak the format.

Step 9: Registration Approval

Once the agency has reviewed your submission and asked you for additional information or clarifications and you've completed all the revisions, they will go through the approval process, at which point your apprenticeship occupation will be approved and registered.

* * *

Well, my friend, that's a wrap! You can see there's a lot of work to be done as a program sponsor. If after reading this you believe you have the capacity internally or you'd like to hire a program sponsor—fantastic. You can still use Apprentix as a tech platform to help you facilitate all the things that we've mentioned to make the process much easier, a lot less bound by red tape, way more efficient, and a lot less likely to cause burnout, leading to a greater likelihood of success for your apprenticeship program.

Or you might've read this and thought, "No way! We're not getting into the business of becoming program sponsors. Let's just join Apprentix's program—they can run our program for us." We're happy to do so. Just contact us, and we'll be happy to work with you to see how we can get this process rolling for you.

Call To Action

Now that you understand all it means to launch an apprenticeship program—how to design one, how to create value, and how to register one—your head might be spinning. *There is so much to do to launch an apprenticeship!* And you're right. But . . . you don't need to solve all of this right now.

Putting thought into *any* component from this book will provide you with a strong foundation to get the process started. The key is that you must act, because you're not going to figure everything out beforehand. Just like an apprentice learns through classroom theory and then hands-on application, reading this book completes your classroom theory. Now it's time to get your hands dirty.

Imagine translating every line of this book into code. That's Apprentix. Your first step might simply be to contact my team and me, or you might start your free thirty-day trial of Apprentix.

If you feel like you're ready to contact my team to see how we can help you launch your apprenticeship, please visit the contact page on our website.

If you're ready to build, go to Apprentix's website and click on "Start for free." The platform itself will guide you every step of the way, and having read this book, you'll know exactly what to do when you get there.

We've covered a lot. I want to make sure that you're prepared and that you're going to be successful in these programs. Too many companies fail at apprenticeship programs, and I want to prevent that from happening to you. It's not a good look for the company, and it's not a good look for the apprentices. Failure is not an option.

And as I've said before . . .

I can't help you make the decision to launch an apprenticeship, but I won't let you fail if you do.

Free Goodies

I'm about to drop a bunch of free stuff in a second—so stick around.

Steve Jobs famously said, "It takes a lot of hard work to make something simple." I spent over 2,500 hours on this book, having written 500+ pages and over a dozen drafts with different frameworks, sequences, and points of focus. In the end, I've distilled this down to what you need to know and written it in plain English without the legalese, academic language, or the psychobabble that plagues the apprenticeship world. All that to say: I hope this work results in you growing your business with great people.

When I look back at my life, helping people grow profit and purpose will be one of the things I'm most proud of. Writing books, teaching courses, building businesses, and even producing music are all ways for me to share what I've learned. My goal is to give you everything I've got, in every format possible, and leave it all on the field.

I wouldn't be able to channel this level of creative energy if I didn't think people would read this book. Your support and enthusiasm make a difference, so thank you for allowing me to do the work that serves my mission.

Every morning when I sit down to work, I say a little prayer: "Dear God, please bless me with your ideas and intuition and guide my fingers to do the work." Without further ado, here is the list of goodies:

1. To get the **free book downloads and training videos** that come with this book, go to **training.apprentix.io/als**.

2. **If you prefer to listen to audiobooks,** I recorded an audio version. You might find it helpful to engrain the lessons by listening to the audiobook while you read. You can get it for free at **training.apprentix.io/als-audiobook**.

3. **If you'd like a customized online demo,** you can get one for free here: **app.apprentix.io/demo**. Select what's important to you, and your demo will automatically be customized so you see what's relevant.

4. **If you'd like a *free trial* of Apprentix,** you can sign up for free with no credit card required. You'll get unlimited access to all the features. Sign up here: **app.apprentix.io**.

5. **If your company has a compelling reason to launch apprenticeships,** schedule your free strategy call here: **Apprentix.io/contact**.

6. **If you are a construction firm looking to win clean energy projects,** I developed an online course to teach you all you need to know about prevailing wages and apprenticeships so you can win these IRA projects. Go here to get the videos: **IRAcompliance.co/clean-energy-apprenticeships**.

7. **If you're struggling with how to run an apprenticeship after it's been launched, my next book will be on operations.** It may or may not be out by the time you read this. It'll be called *Apprenticeship Operating System*™ (*AOS*™). If you search my name, you can find any other books that may be out by the time you read this.

8. This is a little unorthodox, but I care about you as a person too. Here are some other free goodies for you on a personal level:

9. **If you're struggling personally and need practical tools to lift yourself up—** from a place of uncertainty to a place of peace, focus, optimism, energy, and success—get the first chapter of my #1 best-selling book *Bling* for free at **AndySeth.com/bling**.

10. **If you are a music fan or find it easier to remember lyrics than paragraphs**, you can download my album for free at **AndySeth.com/blingthealbum** or listen on any music-streaming service. Just search under my artist name, "A-Luv," for the album *Bling*.

11. **If you enjoy meditating or want to learn a goal-based meditation**, you can listen to my guided meditation here: **AndySeth.com/blingmeditation**.

12. **And if you'd like to stay connected**, let's do so on LinkedIn or X (formerly Twitter): **linkedin.com/in/andyseth** or **x.com/mraseth**.

Thank you one more time. Please be a giver and **share this with other businesses by leaving a review**. It would mean the world to me. Sending you high vibes from my studio.

I hope to meet you and your business soon. Let's get to work.

Andy Seth

Founder of Apprentix

Bibliography

1. Austin, Steven. "The High Cost of Employee Turnover: Causes, Benchmarks, and Reduction Strategies for 2024." Marketing Scoop. May 12, 2024. https://www.marketingscoop.com/marketing/the-high-cost-of-employee-turnover-causes-benchmarks-and-reduction-strategies-for-2024/

2. Campbell, John D., and James V. Reyes-Picknell. *Uptime: Strategies for Excellence in Maintenance Management.* Boca Raton: CRC Press, 1995. https://vdoc.pub/documents/uptime-strategies-for-excellence-in-maintenance-management-2k63kstqup3g.

3. Craig, Ryan. *Apprentice Nation: How the "Earn and Learn" Alternative to Higher Education Will Create a Stronger and Fairer America.* Dallas: BenBella Books, 2023.

4. Daume, Paul. "Renewable-Energy Development in a Net-Zero World: Overcoming Talent Gaps." McKinsey & Company, November 4, 2022. https://www.mckinsey.com/industries/electric-power-and-natural-gas/our-insights/renewable-energy-development-in-a-net-zero-world-overcoming-talent-gaps

5. Education & the Workforce Committee Democrats. "Labor Leaders Introduce Bipartisan Bill to Expand Apprenticeships." News release no. 202-226-0853. April 25, 2023. https://democrats-edworkforce.house.gov/media/press-releases/labor-leaders-introduce-bipartisan-bill-to-expand-apprenticeships.

6. Franklin Apprenticeships. "The Role of Trade Unions in the US Apprenticeship Arena." Transcript of interview with Dr. John Gaal. https://www.franklinapprenticeships.com/role-trade-unions-us-apprenticeship-arena/.

7. Gardiner, Karen, Daniel Kuehn, Elizabeth Copson, and Andrew Clarkwest. *Expanding Registered Apprenticeship in the United States: Description of American Apprenticeship Initiative Grantees and Their Programs.* Report prepared for the US Department of Labor, Employment and Training Administration. Rockville, MD: Abt Associates and Washington, DC: Urban Institute, September 2021. https://www.dol.gov/sites/dolgov/files/OASP/evaluation/pdf/AAI%20Grant%20Program%20Description_Final.pdf.

8. Grant, Adam. *Give and Take: Why Helping Others Drives Our Success*. Penguin Books, 2013. (Referencing UnitedHealth Group's "Doing Good is Good for You: 2013 Health and Volunteering Study")

9. Heinz, Kate. "38 Employee Turnover Statistics to Know." Built In. Last updated by Brennan Whitfield on April 17, 2023. https://builtin.com/recruiting/employee-turnover-statistics.

10. Hoffman, Nancy, and Robert Schwartz. "Gold Standard: The Swiss Vocational Education and Training System." Washington, DC: National Center on Education and the Economy, 2015.

11. House Committee on Education and the Workforce. "National Apprentice Act of 2023." Fact sheet. Ed & Workforce Democrats. https://democrats-edworkforce.house.gov/imo/media/doc/national_apprenticeship_act_of_2023_fact_sheet.pdf#:~:text=URL%3A%20https%3A%2F%2Fdemocrats.

12. "Inflation Reduction Act Will Attract an Extra $270 Billion in US Wind and Solar Investments by 2030." Rystad Energy. August 22, 2022. https://www.rystadenergy.com/news/inflation-reduction-act-will-attract-an-extra-270-billion-in-us-wind-and-solar-in.

13. Lerman, Robert I. "The State of Apprenticeship in the US: A Plan for Scale." Apprenticeships for America. July 2022. https://static1.squarespace.com/static/61f1c7ff7041697cc1eff1bd/t/62d5b4981261b74803071036/1658172568403/planforscale.pdf.

14. Meisels, Michelle, Misha Nikulin, Kate Hardin, Matt Sloane, and Kruttika Dwivedi. "2024 Engineering and Construction Industry Outlook." Deloitte Research Center for Energy & Industrials. November 6, 2023. https://www2.deloitte.com/us/en/insights/industry/engineering-and-construction/engineering-and-construction-industry-outlook.html.

15. Smogluk, Nouran. "16 Alarming Statistics on the Cost of Employee Turnover in 2023." Gomada. https://www.gomada.co/blog/cost-of-employee-turnover-statistics.

16. Wahal, Yashna. "What Is the Cost of Employee Turnover in 2024?" Connecteam. Last updated January 8, 2024. https://connecteam.com/e-cost-of-employee-turnover/.

17. White House. "Biden–Harris Administration Announces Strategies to Train and Connect American Workers to Jobs Created by the President's Investing in America Agenda." Fact sheet. May 16, 2023. https://www.whitehouse.gov/briefing-room/statements-releases/2023/05/16/fact-sheet-biden-harris-administration-announces-strategies-to-train-and-connect-american-workers-to-jobs-created-by-the-presidents-investing-in-america-agenda/.